Anonymous

Ordinances of Salt Lake City passed since December 13th, 1892

Anonymous

Ordinances of Salt Lake City passed since December 13th, 1892

ISBN/EAN: 9783337810788

Printed in Europe, USA, Canada, Australia, Japan

Cover: Foto ©ninafisch / pixelio.de

More available books at **www.hansebooks.com**

OF

SALT LAKE CITY

Passed since December 13th, 1892.

James Jack

PUBLISHED BY AUTHORITY OF THE
CITY COUNCIL OF SALT LAKE CITY, UTAH.
OCTOBER 1, 1894.

ERRATA.

Page 22—Line 9 of Sec. 2 should read as follows: "space between its different rails or tracks, and also a space two".

Page 24—Line 13 of Sec. 1. Insert the word "northwesterly" in lieu of the word "northeasterly".

Page 26—Line 16. Erase the word "of" after the word "statement". Line 17—After the word "estimate" insert the word "at" in lieu of the word "as".

Page 36—Line 13 of Sec. 4. After the word "company" and before the word "making" insert the words "upon such other company".

Page 37—Line 2 of Sec. 7. After the word "city" and before the word "a" insert the words "each year as a special tax, in consideration of the granting of this franchise and in addition to the ordinary property taxes,".

Page 50—Line 14 of Sec. 6. After the word "electric" insert the word "lights".

Page 53—Line 2 of Sec. 6. Insert the word "accident" in lieu of the word "action".

Page 57—Line 4 of Sec. 9. Insert the date "28th" in lieu of the date "24th".

Page 69—Line 5 of Sec. 3. Insert the word "pork," after the word "veal".

Page 75—Line 2 of Sec. 1. Insert the word "pertaining" after the word "duties".

Page 80—Line 12. Insert the word "tamped" in lieu of the word "stamped". Line 19—Insert the word "material" after the word "paving".

Page 81—Line 4. Insert the word "measure" in lieu of the word "manner".

Page 95—Line 12 Insert the figure "3" after the abbreviation "Sec." and in lieu of the figure "2".

Page 103—In line 3, after the word "estate" and before the word "improvements", insert a comma (,).

ORDINANCES

OF

SALT LAKE CITY.

CHAPTER I.

BONDS FOR CORPORATE PURPOSES.

AN ORDINANCE PROVIDING FOR THE ISSUE OF BONDS FOR CORPORATE PURPOSES, FOR $800,000 00.

Whereas, the corporation of Salt Lake City is desirous of borrowing the sum of $800,000.00 for the making of permanent improvements and for other corporate purposes, and it has been deemed prudent and best to issue a series of 800 one-thousand-dollar bonds, pursuant to the provisions of an act of the governor and legislative assembly of the Territory of Utah, approved March 8th, 1888, and amended February 26th, 1894; wherefore,

SECTION 1. Be and it is ordained by the city council of Salt Lake City, that for the purpose of obtaining money for permanent improvements and for other corporate purposes, said corporation shall issue a series of 800 engraved, coupon bonds of the denomination of one thousand dollars each; the principal payable at the office of the city treasurer of the city of Salt Lake City, twenty years after the date thereof.

Said bonds to bear the date of May 1st, 1894, with interest from the date thereof at the rate of five per cent, per annum and payable semi-annually thereafter on the first days of November and May of each year in the city of New York, at the banking house of the National Bank of the Republic, or at the banking house of McCornick & Company of Salt Lake City, or its successors, on the presentation and surrender of the coupons as they become due, both interest and principal payable in gold, and said bonds shall be exempted from taxation by said city.

Sec. 2. Said bonds shall be signed by the mayor and treasurer of said city, and before the issue of any of them the corporate seal of said city shall be thereunto affixed, duly attested by the recorder of said city. The coupons attached to each of the bonds, representing the interest to accrue thereon, shall each be signed by the treasurer of said city, either by his own hand or by lithographic copy of the signature of said treasurer, and such coupons, when so signed, issued and delivered by the proper authorities of said city with such bond or bonds to a purchaser or purchasers thereof, shall become and be lawful obligations of said city in the hands of any person to whom they may lawfully come, for the payment of said interest as shown thereby.

Sec. 3. Said bonds shall be numbered from one to eight hundred, both inclusive, and they shall be registered in numerical order, in a book kept for such purpose by the auditor of said city, and said bonds shall be sold only upon the order of the city council, and in such lots and upon such terms as it shall designate, and to each of said bonds shall be attached forty coupons numbered respectively from one to forty, both inclusive, with the proper date of payment named therein.

Sec. 4. The seal of the corporation shall not be impressed upon said bonds until the sale thereof, and then said impression shall be made in the presence of the mayor, treasurer and committee on finance of said city; provided, the order of selling and attesting said bonds, including the sealing thereof, may be changed or modified by the order of said city council.

Sec. 5. Whenever the city council of Salt Lake City shall have arranged to issue said bonds, or any part of them, said council shall direct the mayor of said city to advertise for the sale of bonds to be issued as aforesaid, by causing notice of said sale to be given in such manner and for such period of time as the city council shall direct. Said notice shall specify the amount of bonds to be sold, rate of interest they shall bear, the place, day and hour of sale, and that the bids shall be received by said mayor, for the purchase of said bonds, and at the place and time named in said notice. The mayor and committee on finance of said city council shall open all bids received by said mayor, and they shall award the purchase of said bonds, or the portion thereof offered for sale, to the highest bidder or bidders therefor; provided, said mayor and said committee on finance shall have the right on behalf of said city to reject any and all bids, and provided further, that they may in their discretion refuse to make any award of said bonds, unless sufficient security shall be furnished by the bidder or bidders for the compliance with the terms of his or their bids.

Sec. 6. For the purpose of providing for the payment of the interest on said bonds as the same shall become due, the sum of twenty thousand dollars semi-annually, or so much thereof as may be necessary, is hereby appropriated accordingly.

At the expiration of ten years after the issuance of said bonds there shall be set apart, and the same is hereby appropriated as a sinking fund, the sum of $80,000 per annum to pay the principal of said bonds when the same shall fall due. Provided, that nothing herein contained shall prevent the city council of Salt Lake City at any time hereafter from making any other provision or appropriation for the redemption of any or all of said bonds, which said provision or appropriation shall be in accordance with the laws of Utah as they now or may hereafter exist.

Seo. 7. This ordinance to take effect from and after its passage.

Passed by the city council of Salt Lake City, Territory of Utah, March 30th, 1894, and referred to the mayor for his approval.
[Approved the 31st day of March, A. D. 1894. Amended April 28th, 1894.]

AN ORDINANCE CONFIRMING THE SALE OF BONDS

SECTION 1. Whereas, by a resolution of this body, duly and regularly passed on the 25th day of July, 1893, the mayor and treasurer were authorized and empowered, in connection with the finance committee, to sell at private sale, all or any part of the 300 bonds of the issue of July 1st, 1892, then remaining in the possession of the city, and numbered from 301 to 600 inclusive; and

Whereas, in pursuance of the authority conferred by said resolution, the mayor, treasurer and finance committee have sold one hundred and twenty-five of said bonds, numbered from 301 to and including 425, to Blair & Co., bankers of the city of New York, and have given option on 125 additional of said bonds; and

Whereas, it was part of the consideration of the said purchasers that an ordinance containing the recitals and provisions of the present ordinance should be passed for the assurance of the said purchasers and all subsequent holders of the said bonds, and that all of the purchase price of said bonds, prior to the delivery of said bonds to said purchasers, shall be actually applied in the retirement and actual cancellation of a like amount of the valid and outstanding warrants of the city; and

Whereas, the aggregate indebtedness of the city of all kinds and for all purposes, including the said issue of bonds sold to said Blair & Co., as aforesaid, did not and does not amount to four per centum of the value of the taxab'e property within the limits of the city, as determined and ascertained by the last assessment for territorial and county taxes, at the date of the delivery of said bonds to Blair & Co.; and

Whereas, all of the provisions of law and ordinances of the said city in respect to the issue and sale of the said bonds have been complied with;

Therefore be it ordained by the city council of the city of Salt Lake that the issuance and sale to Blair & Co. of the bonds aforesaid, and the action of the mayor and finance committee in the premises, be and the same are hereby approved, ratified and confirmed, and the said bonds are declared to be binding and legal obligations upon the city of Salt Lake; and the recorder is directed to furnish a certified copy of this ordinance, under the seal of the city, to the said purchasers of the said bonds or any subsequent holder thereof, as the assurance of the said city that the same are in all respects its binding and legal obligations.

That all ordinances or parts of ordinances in conflict herewith be and the same are hereby repealed.

Sec. 2. That this ordinance shall take effect from and after its approval.

Passed by the city council of Salt Lake City, Territory of Utah, the 6th day of October, 1893, and referred to the mayor for his approval.

[Approved the 6th day of October, A. D. 1893.]

AN ORDINANCE, SUPPLEMENTAL TO AN ORDINANCE PASSED OCTOBER 6TH, 1893, CONFIRMING THE SALE OF BONDS.

Whereas, by a resolution of this body duly and regularly passed on the 25th day of July, 1893, the mayor and treasurer were authorized and empowered in connection with the finance committee, to sell at private sale all or any part of the 300 bonds of the issue of July 1st, 1892, then remaining in the possession of the city and numbered from 301 to 600 inclusive; and

Whereas, in pursuance of the authority conferred by said resolution, the mayor, treasurer and finance committee have in sundry installments, and at various times since the 6th day of October, 1893, sold and delivered 213 of said bonds, numbered from 301 to 513, both inclusive, to Blair & Co., bankers of the city of New York; and

Whereas, it was part of the consideration of said purchase that an ordinance containing the recitals and provisions of the present ordinance should be passed for the assurance of said purchasers and subsequent holders of said bonds; and

Whereas, by the terms of the ordinance of October 6th, 1893, this city agreed to apply the purchase price of said bonds prior to the delivery of said bonds to said purchasers to the retirement and cancellation of a like amount of valid and outstanding warrants of said city, which has since been done by the city, which has applied the proceeds of said bonds numbered from 301 to 513 inclusive, received from Blair & Co., to the cancellation and retirement of valid and outstanding city warrants to an amount at least equal to the bonds so delivered, and which was done before the delivery of the said bonds to Blair & Co.; and

Whereas, the aggregate indebtedness of the city at all times and for all purposes, including the bond sold and delivered to Blair & Co., as aforesaid, did not at the time of the delivery of said bonds or of any installment thereof, amount, and has not at any time since amounted, and does not now amount to four per centum of the value of the taxable property within the said city as determined by the last assessment for territorial and county taxes; and

Whereas, all the provisions of law and of the ordinances of said city in respect to the issue and sale of said bonds, have been complied with, and said Blair & Co. have fully paid the city for said bonds numbered from 301 to 513 inclusive;

Therefore, be it ordained by the city council of the city of Salt Lake, that the issuance and sale to Blair & Co. of the bonds aforesaid, be and the same are hereby approved, ratified and confirmed, and the said bonds numbered from 301 to 513 inclusive, are declared to be binding and legal obligations upon the city of Salt Lake; and the recorder is directed to furnish a certified copy of this ordinance under the seal of the city to said purchasers of the said bonds or any subsequent holders thereof, as the assurance of the said city that the same are in all respects its binding and legal obligations.

That all ordinances or parts of ordinances in conflict herewith be and the same are hereby repealed.

This ordinance shall take effect from and after its approval.

Passed by the city council of Salt Lake City, Territory of Utah, February 27th, 1894, and referred to the mayor for his approval.

[Approved the 28th day of February, A. D. 1894.]

CHAPTER II.

OFFICIAL BONDS.

AN ORDINANCE REQUIRING ALL OFFICERS, CLERKS, OR EMPLOYEES OF SALT LAKE CITY, WHO ARE NOT ALREADY REQUIRED BY LAW TO GIVE BONDS, TO GIVE BONDS BEFORE ENTERING UPON THE DISCHARGE OF THEIR DUTIES.

SECTION 1. Be it ordained by the city council of Salt Lake City, Salt Lake County, Territory of Utah, that all officers, clerks and employees of Salt Lake City, into whose hands any money belonging to the city may come, are, before entering upon their duties as such officer, clerk, or employee, required to give bonds to the city, with sufficient sureties and in such penal sum as may be fixed by and with the approval of the city council.

Sec. 2. This ordinance to be in force from and after its approval.

Passed by the city council of Salt Lake City, Territory of Utah, January 17th, 1893, and referred to the mayor for his approval.

[Approved the 19th day of January, A. D. 1893.]

CHAPTER III.

CLAIMS SWORN TO.

AN ORDINANCE REQUIRING ALL CLAIMS AGAINST THE CITY OF SALT LAKE TO BE SWORN TO.

SECTION 1. Be it ordained by the city council of Salt Lake City, Territory of Utah,

That, after the approval and passage of this ordinance, all claims against the city of Salt Lake, before being presented to the city council for allowance, the party making such claim, or someone in behalf of said party, must make affidavit before the city recorder or his deputy, or any other person authorized to administer oaths, that said claim is correct, that the amount claimed is due and owing, that no part thereof has been previously presented to the council, allowed or paid.

Sec. 2. This ordinance to take effect and be in force from and after its approval.

Passed by the city council of Salt Lake City, Territory of Utah, February 6th, 1894, and referred to the mayor for his approval.

[Approved the 9th day of February, 1894.]

CHAPTER IV.

EMPLOYMENT OFFICE.

AN ORDINANCE, AMENDING SECTION 32, OF CHAPTER XXII., OF THE COMPILED LAWS OF SALT LAKE CITY.

SECTION 1. Be it ordained by the city council of Salt Lake City, Territory of Utah, that Section 32 of Chapter XXII., of the Compiled Ordinances of Salt Lake City, be and the same is hereby amended, by striking out at the end of the fourth line from the bottom of the page 262, of said section, the figures "100" and inserting the figures "60."

See Revised Ordinances p. 262.

Sec. 2. This ordinance shall take effect from and after its approval.

Passed by the city council of Salt Lake City, Territory of Utah, April 14th, 1893, and referred to the mayor for his approval.

[Approved by the mayor April 18th, 1893.]

CHAPTER V.

ENGINEER'S FEES.

AN ORDINANCE, AMENDING SECTION 6, CHAPTER XIV., OF THE ORDINANCES OF SALT LAKE CITY, APPROVED APRIL 1, 1890.

SECTION 6. The city engineer shall be allowed to charge and demand in advance for the benefit of the city, the following fees from the owners of property ordering the work to be performed, or against whom the work is properly chargeable, in all parts of the city over which the official survey shall have been extended, or when the surveys are found to agree substantially with the recorded plats thereof:

For locating the four corners of a rectangular, or nearly rectangular lot of any size, where lines can be run without offsetting	$7 50
For locating one line of a lot of any size, where such line can be run without offsetting	5 50
For each offset made in running a line	50
For each additional course necessary to be run in surveying or subdividing a lot, or surveying a lot of irregular shape	1 00
For establishing building or sidewalk grades for a frontage of twenty-five feet or less	7 00
For establishing building or sidewalk grades for each additional twenty-five feet, or part thereof, on the same block	50

See Revised Ordinances p. 193.

For establishing curb grades for a frontage of
twenty-five feet or less 5 00
For establishing curb grades for each additional
twenty-five feet, or part thereof.   25
For establishing grades for drains, ditches, etc., or for
doing any other surveying work not provided for
above, an amount estimated by the city engineer
to cover actual cost; any excess over actual cost to
be refunded to the party ordering the survey, after
the work shall have been done, and the actual cost
ascertained.

<small>See Revised Ordinances p. 193.</small>

Passed by the city council of Salt Lake City, Territory of Utah, the 15th day of May, 1894, and referred to the mayor for his approval.

[Approved the 19th day of May, A. D. 1894.]

CHAPTER VI.

FIRE DEPARTMENT. NUMBER OF MEN.

AN ORDINANCE, AMENDING AN ORDINANCE ENTITLED "AN ORDINANCE GOVERNING THE SALT LAKE CITY FIRE DEPARTMENT," APPROVED APRIL 29TH, 1890.

SECTION 1. Be it ordained by the city council of Salt Lake City, Territory of Utah, that an ordinance entitled "An Ordinance Governing the Salt Lake City Fire Department," approved April 29th, 1890, be amended to read as follows:

The fire department of Salt Lake City shall consist of a chief of department, one assistant chief, and such other officers and men as such chief shall deem necessary from time to time, but in no case shall the number of permanent men exceed twenty-five.

All officers and men of the fire department shall receive such compensation as may be fixed by order of the city council.

See Revised Ordinances p. 206.

Sec. 2. All ordinances and parts of ordinances in conflict herewith are hereby repealed.

Sec. 3. This ordinance shall take effect and be in force from and after October 1st, 1894.

Passed by the city council of Salt Lake City, Territory of Utah, September 25th, 1894, and referred to the mayor for his approval.

[Approved the 29th day of September, A. D. 1894.]

CHAPTER VII.

INJURY TO FIRE HYDRANTS.

AN ORDINANCE, AMENDING SECTION 4, OF CHAPTER LV., OF THE REVISED ORDINANCES OF SALT LAKE CITY, OF 1892.

SECTION 1. Be it ordained by the city council of Salt Lake City, Territory of Utah, that Sec. 4, of Chapter LV., of the Revised Ordinances of Salt Lake City, of 1892, be and the same is hereby amended by striking out the word "ten," in the last line of said section, and inserting in lieu thereof the word "two."

<small>See Revised Ordinances p. 495.</small>

Sec. 2. This ordinance shall take effect and be in force from and after its approval

Passed by the city council of Salt Lake City. Territory of Utah, September 25th, 1894, and referred to the mayor for his approval.

[Approved the 29th day of September, A. D. 1894.]

CHAPTER VIII.

FRANCHISES.

SALT LAKE CITY RAILROAD COMPANY.

AN ORDINANCE, AMENDING AND RE-ENACTING CERTAIN RESO-
LUTIONS GRANTING FRANCHISES TO THE SALT LAKE CITY RAIL-
ROAD COMPANY.

Whereas, the Salt Lake City Railroad Company is the owner of certain lines of street railway in the city of Salt Lake, and is and has been engaged in the operation of the same under and by virtue of certain resolutions and ordinances hereinafter more particularly described; and

Whereas, questions have heretofore arisen between the city and said railroad company, respecting the duties and obligations of said company as to the payment of license-tax and the paving and repaving of the streets upon which said lines of railroad are constructed; and

Whereas, the said company has heretofore requested this council to grant to it an extension of the rights and privileges by it had and enjoyed under said resolutions and ordinances.

Now, therefore, for the purpose of determining the questions which have arisen between the city and said company, as aforesaid, and of fixing the liability and duties of said company in the premises,

Be it ordained, by the mayor and city council of Salt Lake City, as follows, to-wit:

SECTION 1. That certain resolutions heretofore passed and adopted by the mayor and city council of Salt Lake City, granting rights and privileges for the construction and operation of a line or lines of street railway upon the streets of Salt Lake City, to-wit:

Resolutions granting franchises to the Salt Lake City Railroad Company, passed and adopted February 26th, 1889; February 11th, 1890; May 20th, 1890; September 23rd, 1890; May 5th 1891; September 8th, 1891; November 24th, 1891; and resolutions granting a franchise to L. C. Hamilton, passed and adopted January 20th, 1891, be and each of them is amended by striking out from section 2 of each of said resolutions the words "of twenty (20) years from the date of the passage of this resolution," and substituting in lieu thereof the words "of fifty (50) years from January 1st, A. D., 1894."

Sec. 2. And said resolutions and each of them are further amended by striking out from the first section of each of said resolutions the provision requiring the grantee to pay into the city treasury a per capita tax of one and one-fourth (1¼) mills for each and every fare collected wherever the same may occur, and by inserting in lieu of such provision the following, to-wit:

"The said grantee shall pay into the city treasury annually a license tax of twenty-five ($25) dollars per car for the average number of motor cars operated upon its lines, but otherwise said company shall not be liable to any per capita tax or license."

But this clause shall not be deemed as an exemption of said company from paying the regular territorial, county, school and municipal taxes as the same may be levied or assessed.

Sec. 3. That the resolutions mentioned in section 1 of this ordinance be and the same are hereby amended by inserting therein the following provisions, to wit:

"Said company shall be required to pave or repave, at its own expense and cost, all space between its different rails or tracks, and also a space two feet wide on the outside of the rails of the outside tracks, and the tracks herein referred to shall include not only the main tracks but also all side track, crossings and turn-outs used by said company. Such paving or repaving by the said railroad company shall be at the same time and shall be of the same material and character as are proper for the repaving of the streets or alleys on which said railroad track or tracks are paved and located, unless other material be specially ordered by the board of public works. Provided, that where the said company has double tracks on the same street and it be required, for the accommodation of some other corporation or person, to lay its tracks a greater distance apart than it would be required to do but for the accommodation of such other corporation or person, then in that event the said railroad company shall not be liable for or required to pave such additional distance."

Sec. 4. The price of a single passage within the city limits shall not exceed five cents, and no charge shall be made in excess thereof excepting where the passage or some portion thereof shall be over any part of the line of the grantee lying within the limits of Fort Douglas military reservation, so long as said reservation shall exist, and in case its boundaries shall hereafter be reduced in area, the above exception shall apply only to such area.

Sec. 5. The grantee shall be liable for all accidents to people or injury to property whether of the city or private parties in the construction and operation of its said railroad, occasioned by its misconduct, negligence or default, and particularly in the use of electricity thereon, and the said company shall at all times be required to use such reasonable and approved methods as are then in successful use by cities of approximately the same size as Salt Lake City, and as shall at any time be requested by the city council and the board of public works for the protection of the public and its property against injury caused by the use of electricity as motive power; and if deemed necessary by the said city council and board of public works the said company shall have, make and maintain a complete metallic circuit of such approved kind as shall be used and adopted and proven by experience to be proper and reasonable.

Sec. 6. The rights and privileges hereby given and all restrictions and limitations herein contained shall be deemed a part of and run with this grant and sh ll be operative so long as the privileges and franchises herein given shall exist, and in case the corporate limits of the city shall in the future be extended, all the lines of said company, within the corporate boundary as so enlarged, shall become and be subject to the terms and conditions of the charters of said company, as amended by this ordinance, the same as if said lines were now within the corporate limits.

Sec. 7. That all ordinances, resolutions and parts thereof, in conflict with the provisions of this ordinance, are hereby repealed, and the resolutions mentioned in section 1 of this ordinance, amended as herein provided, are hereby re-enacted and made operative from the date of the passage of this ordinance.

Sec. 8. If this grant be not accepted in writing by the grantee, within twenty days after the passage of this ordinance, the same shall become void and of no effect.

Passed by the city council the 17th day of April, A. D. 1894, and referred to the mayor for his approval.

[Approved the 18th day of April, 1894.]

SALT LAKE RAPID TRANSIT COMPANY.

AN ORDINANCE, EXTENDING, REGRANTING AND CONFIRMING CERTAIN RESODUTIONS AND ORDINANCES HERETOFORE PASSED BY THE CITY COUNCIL OF SALT LAKE CITY, GRANTING FRANCHISES TO THE SALT LAKE RAPID TRANSIT COMPANY, THE POPPERTON PLACE AND FORT DOUGLAS RAPID TRANSIT COMPANY AND TO C. E WANTLAND AND OTHERS, AND AMENDING THE SAME

Whereas, the Salt Lake Rap'd Transit Company is operating a system of street railway in Salt Lake City, including therein the railway lines of the Popperton Place and Fort Douglas Rapid Transit Company and the East Bench Street Railway Company, (successors to C. E. Wantland and others), the right to construct and operate the said railways having been acquired by several franchises granted by the city council of said city, and the county court of Salt Lake County, varying in limit of time and the method of computing the license tax paid to the city ; and,

Whereas, questions have arisen between the city and said company respecting the duties and obligations of said company as to the amount of special or license tax to be paid by said company, and in respect to the paving and repaving of the streets upon which the lines of railway of said company are constructed: and,

Whereas, the said company has requested the council to grant to it an extension of the rights and privileges by it had and enjoyed under said resolutions and ordinances ;

Now, therefore, for the purpose of settling and determining the questions which have heretofore arisen between the said city and the said company, as aforesaid, and of fixing the liability and duty of the said company in the premises :

Be it hereby ordained by the city council of Salt Lake City as follows, to-wit :

SECTION 1. That the rights and privileges conferred by the several ordinances or resolutions of said city council and the county court of Salt Lake County, heretofore passed, granting franchises to the Salt Lake Rapid Transit Company, the said Popperton Place and Fort Douglas Rapid Transit Company, and the said C. E. Wantland and others, and the amendments thereto be and the same are hereby regranted and extended for the period of fifty years from the first day of January, 1894, upon the terms and under the conditions, restrictions and limitations contained in the resolution of February 11th, 1890, except as modified hereby, subject, however, to the following modifications and provisions, to-wit :

The said grantee shall pay into the city treasusy, annually, a license tax of $25 per car for the average number of motor cars operated upon its line, but otherwise said company shall not be liable for any per capita tax or license; but this clause shall not be deemed an exemption of the said company from paying the regular territorial, county, school and municipal taxes as the same may be levied or assessed.

Sec. 2. That the resolutions mentioned in section 1 of this ordinance be and the same are amended by inserting therein the following provisions, to-wit:

Said company shall be required to move its track on North Temple street, between Main and State streets, to the north side of the conduit, in accordance with the resolution of the city council, adopted March 20th, 1894; and said company shall be required to pave or repave, at its own expense and cost, all the space between its different rails and tracks, or also a space two feet wide on the outside of the rails of the outside tracks, and the tracks herein referred to shall include not only the main tracks but also the side tracks, crossings and turnouts used by said company; such paving or repaving by the said railroad company shall be at the same time and shall be of the same material and character as are proper for the repaving of the streets or alleys on which the said railroad track or tracks are paved and located, unless other material be specially ordered by the board of public works; provided, that where the said company has double tracks on the same street, and it be required for the accommodation of some other corporation or person to lay its tracks a greater distance apart than it would be required to do but for the accommodation of such other corporation or person, then, in that event, the said railroad company shall not be liable for or required to pave said additional distance.

Sec. 3. The price of a single passage shall not exceed five cents, and no charge shall be made in excess thereof within said city, excepting where the passage, or some portion thereof, shall be over any part of the line of the grantee lying within the limits of the Fort Douglas military reservation, so long as this reservation shall exist, and in case its boundaries shall hereafter be reduced in area, the above exception shall apply only to such area.

Sec 4. The grantee shall be liable for all accidents to persons or injury to property, whether of the city or private parties, in the construction and operation of its railroad in consequence of its misconduct or default, and particularly in the use of electricity thereon; and the said company shall at all times be required to use such reasonable and approved methods as are then in successful use by cities of approximately the same size as Salt Lake City and as shall at any time be requested by the city council and the board of public works for the protection of the public and its property against injury caused by the use of electricity as a motive power; and if deemed necessary by the said city council and the board of public works, the said company shall have, make and maintain a complete metallic circuit of such approved kind as shall be used and adopted and proven by experience to be proper and reasonable.

Sec. 5. The rights and privileges hereby given and all restrictions and limitations herein contained shall be deemed a part of and shall run with this grant and shall be operative so long as the privileges and franchises herein given shall exist; and in case the corporate limits of the city shall in the future be extended, all the line of said company within the corporate boundary so enlarged shall become and be subject to the terms and conditions of said charters as amended by this ordinance, the same as if said lines were now within the corporate limits.

Sec. 6. That all ordinances, resolutions and parts thereof in conflict with the provisions of this ordinance are hereby repealed, and the resolutions mentioned in section 1 of this ordinance, amended as herein provided, are hereby re-enacted and made operative from the date of the passage of this ordinance.

Sec. 7. If this grant be not accepted in writing by the grantee within twenty days after the passage of this ordinance, the same shall become void and of no effect.

Passed by the city council this 17th day of April, A. D. 1894, and referred to the Mayor for his approval.

[Approved the 18th day of April, A. D. 1894.]

H. M. M'CARTNEY ET AL.

A RESOLUTION GRANTING A FRANCHISE TO H. M. M'CARTNEY, SAM J. KENYON, S F. WALKER AND S. V. TRENT FOR AN ELECTRIC OR CABLE RAILWAY.

SECTION 1. Be it resolved by the city council of Salt Lake City that H. M. McCartney, Sam J. Kenyon, S. F. Walker and S. V. Trent, their successors and assigns, have the authority and consent of the city council and the permission is hereby granted them to construct and operate by electric or cable motive power, a single track railway, with the necessary switches and turnouts, on the following streets of Salt Lake City, namely:

Commencing at the intersection of State street and South Capitol street, thence east on South Capitol street to its intercection with East Capitol street, thence northward on East Capitol street to its intersection with Paris avenue, the northern boundary of plat J, thence northeasterly along the side hill to the northern boundary of Salt Lake City in the western part of section 13, township 1 north, range 1 west, on the following conditions, to wit:

Such track to be laid on such grades as are now or may be hereafter established by the city council. In consideration of this franchise the grantees, their successors and assigns aforesaid, are required to pave and keep in good repair, at their own cost, with the same material and in the same manner as the rest of the street is or may be paved, all the space inside the tracks, and a space of two feet on each side of the same, including all spaces between double tracks, whether the tracks shall be straight, curved, parallel or otherwise. And the grantees aforesaid shall place cars upon said railway with all necessary modern improvements for the convenience and comfort of passengers, which shall be run thereon each and every day both ways as often as the public convenience may require, and at a rate of speed not exceeding twelve miles an hour, and under such regulations as the city council may from time to time prescribe; provided that the grantees aforesaid shall comply with the directions of the city council in the construction of the said railway and switches, and in any other matter connected with the regulation of the same, and that the track or tracks shall be constructed in the center of the streets, unless otherwise directed by the city council and in such manner as shall be approved by the street supervisor; the track to be laid and road operated so as to cause no unnecessary impediment to the common and ordinary use of said street for all purposes, and that the water courses of said streets be left free and unobstructed; said track to be laid upon a good foundation, even with the surface of the roadway, and whenever streets shall be paved flat rails shall be used on such streets, same to be approved by the city council, and that good and permanent crossings shall be made by the grantees aforesaid at the intersections of the streets and elsewhere, wherever the same shall be necessary, at the discretion of the city council, and under the direction and to the acceptance of the street supervisor. The price of a single passage within the city limits shall not exceed ten (10) cents, and no charge shall be made in excess thereof; the rate of fare, however, to be subject to further regulation at any time by the city council. And the said grantees and their assigns shall pay into the city treasury on the last day of December, 1891, and annually thereafter, a license tax of a sum equal to one-half of one per centum of the gross earnings of the said railway for the first five years of the life of this franchise; one per centum of the gross earnings of said railway for the following five years; one and one-half per centum of the gross earnings of said railway for the following five years, and two per centum of the gross earnings of said railway for the remainder of the life of this franchise. That the company shall on the last day of December, 1894 and the last day of December each year thereafter, file with the recorder of the city an itemized statement, verified by the oath of the president or superintendent of the company, showing accurately the gross earnings of the company for the year immediately preceding the date of such statement, and if the lines of street railway in this charter granted shall be run or operated in connection with any road beyond the corporate limits, all tickets for passage over such line beyond the corporate limits, over any such roads, in fixing in said statement of the amount of such gross earnings, shall be taken and estimated as the same amount as the company shall for tickets within the corporate limits, charge passengers, and in case the corporate limits shall in future be extended, all the lines of the company within such boundary as extended, shall become and be subject to the terms and conditions of this charter, the same as if now within the corporate limits. The said grantees shall provide and maintain at their own cost a group or series of five (5) incandescent lights at all steam railway crossings and other dangerous points on their road, and all such lights shall be kept burning during such hours in the night as their cars shall be in operation.

Sec. 2 That this franchise is granted for the term of twenty-five (25) years from the date of the passage of this resolution, and accepted on the following conditions, viz.: That if the grantees, their successors and assigns, shall fail to perform all or any of the stipulations of this resolution, the city council, after sixty (60) days' notice, and on failure on the part of the said grantees to provide a remedy or make satisfactory arrangements therefor, may, by a two-thirds vote, declare the privileges herein granted forfeited, and proceed to take possession of the roadbed, and control the same as if this resolution had not been passed.

Sec. 3. That nothing in this grant shall be construed as to prevent from paving, sewering, laying gas or water pipes, altering, repairing or in any manner improving any of the streets mentioned herein, or any other streets of said city; but all such improvements shall be made with as little injury as practicable to said railway and the operating thereof.

Sec. 4. That in the construction and operating of said railway, the said grantees and their successors and assigns, shall at all times conform to such ordinances, rules and regulations as have been or hereafter may be adopted by said city council of said city in relation to operating electric or cable street railways in said city, and for each violation thereof they shall be liable to a fine in any sum not exceeding one hundred dollars. That whenever the city council shall grant to any other person or company a franchise for a railway over or along any of the streets herein granted, and it shall be necessary in the opinion of said council to secure to such other persons or company a connection with any important center or terminus without increasing the number of tracks, then the grantees herein shall allow running arrangements over grantees' tracks to such other persons or company making equitable payment for constructing, maintaining and operating the portion of said grantees' tracks so used.

Sec. 5. That Salt Lake City shall in no way be liable or responsible for any accident or damage that may occur in the construction or operation of raid railway by reason of the default or misconduct of the grantee and its successors and assigns, or their employees, and the acceptance of this grant shall be deemed an agreement on the part of said grantees, for themselves and their successors and assigns to save the said city harmless from and against all liability, loss, cost, expense or damage of any nature arising out of any such default, or misconduct, or which may accrue by reason of any accident or injury which may occur in or by reason of the construction or operation of said railway, and to indemnify and repay said city for any loss, cost, expense or damage of any kind it may sustain by reason of such default, misconduct, accident or injury; and if any judgment for damages for such default, misconduct, accident or injury shall be recovered against said city, the recovery thereof and the judgment therefor shall be final as between the said city and the said grantees and their successors and assigns, and conclusive as to the liability of the latter to the former; provided, said grantees have had notice of the pendency of the suit in which said judgment is recovered and have been given an opportunity to defend the same.

Sec. 6. That if this grant, with the terms and conditions therein contained, be not accepted in writing by the said grantees within thirty (30) days after the passage of this resolution, or if the work be not commenced within six (6) months after said acceptance, this grant to become null and void; and as to all streets herein granted upon which the road shall not be completed and in operation within twenty (20) months after the date of said acceptance, this grant to become null and void.

Passed by the city council of Salt Lake City, Territory of Utah, December 26th, 1893, and referred to the mayor for his approval.

[Approved the 30th day of December, A. D. 1893.]

WM H. ROWE, ET AL.

A RESOLUTION GRANTING A FRANCHISE TO WILLIAM H. ROWE, R. M. JONES, JOSEPH W. SUMMERHAYS AND GEORGE M. CANNON, FOR AN ELECTRIC RAILWAY.

SECTION 1. Be it resolved by the city council of Salt Lake City: That William H. Rowe, R. M. Jones, Joseph W. Summerhays and George M. Cannon, their successors and assigns, have the authority and consent of the city council, and the permission is hereby granted them, to construct and operate by electric motive power a single track electric railway on all streets less than eight rods wide, and a double track electric railway on all streets which are eight rods or more in width, together with all the necessary switches for the accommodation of said road, on the following streets of Salt Lake City, namely:

First—Commencing at the intersection of Second East street and First South street, in Salt Lake City, Utah, and running thence south along the said Second East street to the intersection of Ninth South street, thence running east along said Ninth South street to the intersection of Third East Street, thence south along said Third East street to Tenth South street, thence east along said Tenth South street to Seventh East street, thence south along Seventh East street to the city limits.

Second—Commencing at the intersection of Ninth South street and Second East street, and running thence west to Sixth West street, on the following conditions, viz.: Such track or tracks to be laid on such grades as are now or may be hereafter established by the city council. In consideration of this franchise the grantees, their successors and assigns as aforesaid, are hereby required to pave and keep in good repair, at their own cost, with the same material and in the same manner as the rest of the street is or may be paved, all the space inside the tracks, and a space of two feet each side of the same, including all spaces between double tracks, whether the tracks shall be straight, curved, parallel or otherwise. And the grantees aforesaid shall place cars upon said railway with all necessary modern improvements for the convenience and comfort of passengers, which shall be run thereon each and every day both ways, as often as the public convenience may require, and at a rate of speed not exceeding twelve miles an hour, and under such regulations as the city council may from time to time prescribe; provided, that the grantees aforesaid shall comply with the directions of the city council in the construction of the said railway and its switches, and in any other matter connected with the regulation of the same, and that the track or tracks shall be constructed in the center of the streets, unless otherwise directed by the city council, and in such manner as shall be approved by the street supervisor, and that the trolley wire shall be suspended; the track to be laid and the road operated so as to cause no unnecessary impediment to the common and ordinary use of said street for all purposes, and that the water courses of said streets be left free and unobstructed; said track to be laid upon a good foundation, even with the surface of the roadway, and whenever streets shall be paved flat rails shall be used on such streets, same to be approved by the city council, and that good and permanent crossings shall be made by the grantees aforesaid at the intersections of the streets and elsewhere, wherever the same shall be necessary, at the discretion of the city council, and under the direction and to the acceptance of the street upervisor. The price of a single passage within the city limits shall not exceed five (5) cents, and no charge shall be made in excess thereof. And the said grantees and their assigns shall pay into the city treasury on the last day of December, 1894, and annually thereafter, a license tax of a sum equal to one-half of one per centum of the gross earnings of said railway for the first five years of the life of this franchise; one per centum of the gross earnings of said railway for the following five years; one and one-half per centum of the gross earnings of said railway for the following five years; and two per centum of the gross earnings of said railway for the remainder of the life of this franchise. That the company shall on the last day of December, 1894, and the last day of December each year thereafter, file with the recorder of the city an itemized statement, verified by the oath of the president or superintendent of the company, showing accurately the gross earnings of the company for the year immediately preceding the date of such statement, and if the lines of street railway in this charter granted shall be run or operated in connection with any road beyond the corporate limits, all tickets for passage over such line beyond the corporate limits, over any such roads, in fixing in said statement the amount of such gross earnings, shall be taken and estimated at the same amount as the company shall for tickets within corporate limits, charge passengers, and in case the corporate limits shall in the future be extended, all the lines of the company within such boundary as extended, shall become and be subject to the terms and conditions of this charter, the same as if now within the corporate limits. The said grantees shall provide and maintain at their own cost a group or series of five (5) incandescent lights at all steam railway crossings and other dangerous points on their road, and all such lights shall be kept burning during such hours of the night as their cars shall be in operation.

Sec. 2. That this franchise is granted for the term of twenty-five (25) years from the date of the passage of this resolution, and accepted on the following conditions, viz.: That if the grantees, their successors and assigns, shall fail to perform all or any of the stipulations of this resolution, the city council, after sixty (60) days' notice, and on failure on the part of said grantees to provide a remedy or make satisfactory arrangements therefor, may, by a two-thirds vote, declare the privileges herein granted forfeited, and proceed to take possession of the road-bed, and control the same as if this resolution had not been passed.

Sec. 3. That nothing in this grant shall be construed as to prevent from paving, sewering, laying gas or water pipes, altering, repairing or in any manner improving any of the streets mentioned herein, or any other streets of said city; but all such improvements shall be made with as little injury as practicable to said railway and the operating thereof.

Sec. 4. That in the construction and operation of said railway, the said grantees and their, successors and assigns, shall at all times conform to such ordinances, rules and regulations as have been or hereafter may be adopted by said city council of said city in relation to operating electric street railways in said city, and for each violation thereof they shall be liable to a fine in any sum not exceeding one hundred dollars. That whenever the city council shall grant to any other person or company a franchise for a railway over or along any of the streets herein granted, and it shall be necessary in the opinion of said council to secure to such other persons or company a connection with any important center or terminus without increasing the number of tracks, then the grantees herein shall allow running arrangements over grantees' tracks to such other persons or company making equitable payment for constructing, maintaining and operating the portion of said grantees' tracks so used.

Sec. 5. That Salt Lake City shall in no way be liable or responsible for any accident or damage that may occur in the construction or operation of said railway by reason of the default or misconduct of the grantee and its successors and assigns, or their employees, and the acceptance of this grant shall be deemed an agreement on the part of said grantees, for themselves and their successors and assigns, to save the said city harmless from and against all liability, loss, cost, expense or damage of any nature arising out of any such default or misconduct, or which may accrue by reason of any accident or injury which may occur in or by reason of the construction or operation of said railway, and to indemnify and repay said city for any loss, cost, expense or damage of any kind, it may sustain by reason of such default, misconduct accident or injury; and if any judgment for damages for such default, misconduct, accident or injury shall be recovered against said city, the recovery thereof and the judgment therefor shall be final as between the said city and the said grantees and their successors and assigns, and conclusive as to the liability of the latter to the former; provided, said grantees have had notice of the pendency of the suit in which said judgment is recovered and have been given an opportunity to defend the same.

Sec. 6. That if this grant, with the terms and conditions therein contained, be not accepted in writing by the said grantees within thirty (30) days after the passage of this resolution, or if the work be not commenced within six (6) months after said acceptance, this grant to become null and void: and as to all streets herein granted upon which the road shall not be completed and in operation within twenty (20) months after the date of said acceptance, this grant to become null and void.

Passed and referred to the mayor for his approval December 1st, 1893.

[Approved the 2nd day of December, 1893.]

OTTO STALLMAN ET AL.

A RESOLUTION GRANTING A FRANCHISE TO OTTO STALLMAN AND STEPHEN A. ESTES FOR A STREET RAILWAY.

SECTION 1. Be it resolved by the city council of Salt Lake City: That Otto Stallman and Stephen A. Estes, their successors and assigns, have the authority and consent of the city council, and the permission is hereby granted them, to construct and operate by electric or cable motive power, a single or double track railroad, together with all the necessary switches for the accommodation of said road, on the following streets of said city, namely:

First.—Commencing at the Warm Springs and running thence northwesterly along the county road to the intersection of the county road with Ninth North street; thence running west along Ninth North street to the intersection of Ninth North street with Marion boulevard; thence north along Marion boulevard to the intersection of Marion boulevard with Everett street; thence west along Everett street to the west line of the Kinney & Gourlay improved city plat; thence west along the proposed continuation of Everett street, to be dedicated to the public as a street, to the intersection of the proposed Amos avenue, also to be dedicated to the public as a street, with Everett street; thence north along the proposed Amos avenue into Amos avenue as now on record in Kinney's Copper Plant Subdivision No. 2; thence north along Amos avenue to the intersection of Amos avenue with Blucher street; thence west along Blucher street to the west line of Kinney's Copper Plant Subdivision No. 1.

Second.—Commencing at the intersection of Third West and Fourth North street, thence running west along Fourth North street to the intersection of Ninth West street and Fourth North street; thence north along Ninth West street to the intersection of Ninth West street and Ninth North street.

On the following conditions, viz.: Such track or tracks to be laid on such grades as are now or may be hereafter established by the city council. In consideration of this franchise the grantees, their successors and assigns as aforesaid, are hereby required to pave and keep in good repair, with the same material and in the manner as the rest of the street is or may be paved, the space inside the tracks, and a space two feet each side of the same, including all spaces between double tracks where the same may be constructed, and to use no steam power, unless the same be stationary, on any part of the road for propelling cars, unless permitted by the city council. And the grantees aforesaid shall place cars upon said railroad with all necessary modern improvements for the convenience and comfort of passengers, which shall be run thereon each and every day both ways, as often as the public convenience may require, and at a rate of speed not exceeding twelve miles an hour, and under such regulations as the city council may from time to time prescribe; provided, that the grantees aforesaid shall comply with the directions of the city council in the construction of the said railroad and its switches, and in any other matter connected with the regulation of the same, and that the track or tracks shall be constructed in the center of the streets, unless otherwise directed by the city council, and in such a manner as shall be approved by the street supervisor, and that the trolley wire (if electricity be used) shall be suspended from wires attached to poles at or near the curb line of the street; the track to be laid and the road operated so as to cause no unnecessary impediment to the common and ordinary use of said street for all purposes, and that the water courses of said streets be left free and unobstructed; said track to be laid upon a good foundation, even with the surface of the roadway, and whenever streets shall be paved flat rails shall be used on such streets, and that good and permanent crossings shall be made by the grantees aforesaid at the intersections of streets and elsewhere, wherever the same shall be necessary, at the discretion of the city council, and under the direction and to the acceptance of the street upervisor. The price of a single passage shall not exceed five cents, and no charge shall be made in excess thereof.

Sec. 2. That this franchise is granted for the term of twenty-five years from the date of the passage of this resolution, and accepted on the following conditions, viz.: That if the grantees, their successors and assigns, shall fail to perform all or any of the stipulations of this resolution, the city council, after sixty days' notice, and on failure on the part of said grantees to provide a remedy or make satisfactory arrangements therefor, may, by a two-thirds vote, declare the privileges herein granted forfeited, and proceed to take possession of the road-bed, and control the same as if this resolution had not been passed.

Sec. 3. That nothing in this grant shall be so construed as to prevent Salt Lake City or its authorized agents from paving, sewering, laying gas or water mains or pipes, altering, repairing or in any manner improving any of the streets mentioned herein, or any other streets of said city; but all such improvements shall be made with as little injury as practicable to said railway and the operating thereof.

Sec. 4. That in the construction and operation of said railway, the said grantees and their successors and assigns, shall at all times conform to such ordinances, rules and regulations as have been or hereafter may be adopted by said city council of said city in relation to operating railroads, street railways or tramways in said city, and for each violation thereof they shall be liable to a fine in any sum not exceeding one hundred dollars. That whenever the city council shall find it necessary or desirable to grant to any other street railroad company a franchise over any of the streets herein granted, to secure to such other company a connection with any important center or terminus the grantees herein shall allow running arrangements over grantees' tracks to such other company making equitable payment for constructing, maintaining and operating the portion of said grantees' tracks so used.

Sec. 5. That Salt Lake City shall in no way be liable or responsible for any accident or damage that may occur in the construction or operation of said railway by reason of the default or misconduct of the grantee and its successors and assigns, or their employees, and the acceptance of this grant shall be deemed an agreement on the part of said grantees, for themselves and their successors and assigns, to save the said city harmless from and against all liability, loss, cost, expense or damage of any nature arising out of any such default or misconduct, or which may accrue by reason of any accident or injury which may occur in or by reason of the construction or operation of said railway, and to indemnify and repay said city for any loss, cost, expense or damage of any kind, it may sustain by reason of any such default, misconduct, accident or injury; and if any judgment for damages for any such default, misconduct, accident or injury shall be recovered against said city, the recovery thereof and the judgment therefor shall be final as between the said city and the said grantees and their successors and assigns, and conclusive as to the liability of the latter to the former; provided, said grantees have had notice of the pendency of the suit in which said judgment is recovered and have been given an opportunity to defend the same.

Sec. 6. That if this grant, with the terms and conditions therein contained, be not accepted in writing by said grantees on or before December 15th, 1893, or if work be not commenced on or before May 31st, 1894, and the line commencing at the Warm Springs and running northwesterly along the county road to its intersection with Ninth North street, thence running west along Ninth North street to its intersection with Marion boulevard, thence north along Marion boulevard to its intersection with Everett street and said line commencing at the intersection of Third West street and Fourth North streets, and thence running west along Fourth North street to the intersection of Ninth West street, thence north along Ninth West street to its intersection by Ninth North street completed within ten (10) months after commencing said work, this grant shall become null and void.

Sec. 7. The said grantees and their assigns shall pay into the treasury of the city a sum equal to one-half of one per centum of the gross earnings of said railway for the first five years of the life of this franchise; one per centum of the gross earnings of said railway for the following five years; and one and one-half per centum of the gross earnings of said railway for the remainder of the life of this franchise. And for the purpose of enabling the city to arrive at the amount of said special tax, said company shall, on the first day of January of each year, file with the Recorder of said city a report verified by the oath of some officer of said company showing in detail the gross earnings of said railway company from all sources for the year next preceding the date of the filing of such report and said special tax shall be due and payable on the filing of such report.

Passed by the City Council of Salt Lake City, Territory of Utah, August 8th, 1893, and referred to the Mayor for his approval.

[Approved the 10th day of August, 1893.
[Amended December 23rd, 1893.]

SALT LAKE & LOS ANGELES RAILWAY COMPANY.

AN ORDINANCE AMENDING "AN ORDINANCE GRANTING A RIGHT OF WAY THROUGH CERTAIN STREETS OF SALT LAKE CITY FOR A RAILROAD TO THE SALTAIR RAILWAY COMPANY, ITS SUCCESSORS AND ASSIGNS."

Be it ordained by the city council of Salt Lake City: That an ordinance of said city entitled an "Ordinance granting a right of way through certain streets of Salt Lake City for a railroad to the Saltair Railway Company, its successors and assigns," passed January 19th, 1892, be, and the same is hereby amended so that the first part of section one of said ordinance down to the paaagraph in said section beginning with the word "First" shall read as follows:

See Revised Ordinances, p. 329.

SECTION 1. Be it ordained by the city council of Salt Lake City: That the Salt Lake and Los Angeles Railway Company, its successors and assigns, have the authority and consent of the city council, and the permission is hereby granted, to construct and operate a single track standard guage railroad, together with all the necessary switches for the accommodation of said road, to propel thereon cars by steam power, on the following streets of said city: Commencing at a point in South Temple street on the western boundary of said city, where said company's railroad now crosses said boundary, and extending east along said South Temple street from the western limit of city to a point near Fourth West street and thence curving south across said South Temple street and Fourth West street and the sidewalks thereof, into block eighty (80), plat "A," Salt Lake City survey; also the right to construct a curve to connect with the Utah Central Railway Company's track on Fourth West street: provided, that said railroad shall be constructed on South Temple street from the west side of Sixth West street to Fourth West street on the ground now occupied by the Rio Grande Western Railway track and that the temporary right of way heretofore granted to the Denver & Rio Grande Railway Company, now the Rio Grande Western Railway Company, be, and the same is hereby revoked, and that the said Rio Grande Western Railway Company shall have a right of way, during the term of this franchise, over the said track of the Salt Lake and Los Angeles Railway company from said Sixth West street to Fourth West street, without charge, for the purposes for which said track is now used by the said Rio Grande Western Railway Company and neither of said companies shall unnecessarily interfere with the business of the other company nor in any way delay the trains on said road; and the said Salt Lake and Los Angeles Railway Company shall put in and maintain all necessary crossings affected by this grant

See Revised Ordinances, p. 329.

Passed by the City Council of Salt Lake City, Territory of Utah, the 27th day of April, A. D. 1894, and referred to the Mayor for his approval.

[Approved the third day of May, A. D. 1894.]

S. F. WALKER.

AN ORDINANCE GRANTING A FRANCHISE TO S. F. WALKER, HIS HEIRS AND ASSIGNS.

Be it ordained by the City Council of Salt Lake City, Territory of Utah:

SECTION 1. That S. F. Walker, his heirs and assigns, have the authority and consent of the City Council of said city, and the permission is hereby granted to him, his heirs and assigns, to use and occupy the streets, lanes, alleys and public places of said city for the right and privilege of conveying gas and electric currents by means of suitable pipes or conduits to be laid below the surface of the ground; or by means of wires or conductors placed above said streets to be used for electrical lighting and the furnishing of power, and also by means of pipes laid below the surface of the ground for conveying steam for heating, furnishing power and other purposes to the inhabitants, property owners and users in said city for the term of twenty-five (25) years from and after the date of the passage of this ordinance.

SEC. 2. That said S. F. Walker, his heirs and assigns, during said term be, and they are hereby vested with the right and privilege of entering upon the streets, lanes, alleys and public places of said city for the following purposes, viz:

First—The opening of said streets, lanes, alleys and public places for the purpose of laying gas mains, electrical conduits or pipes for steam purposes.

Second—The privilege of erecting and maintaining in the streets, lanes, alleys and public places of said city poles and attaching thereto and maintaining thereon wires and conductors for the purpose of transmitting electrical currents within the limits of the said city to the inhabitants thereof.

Sec. 3. That said S. F. Walker, his heirs and assigns, shall file with the city engineer a plat showing the streets, lanes, alleys and public places where it is proposed to locate gas or steam pipes and electrical conduits and erect poles. And the said grantee, his heirs and assigns, shall have the right to open trenches for the purpose of laying said mains, pipes and conduits, and that no pipes or conduits shall be laid nearer than two feet from any water main or sewer pipe, except in crossing the same; and for the purpose of maintaining them in good repair, the said grantee, his heirs and assigns, to have access to all such mains, gas or steam pipes or conduits as may be necessary from time to time.

Sec. 4. All streets, lanes, alleys and public places that may be opened by said grantee, his successors and assigns, for the aforesaid purposes shall be filled in and put in as good repair and order as they were before being opened, and within a reasonable time, so as not to unnecessarily obstruct the free passage over the streets. That the opening of streets and the erection of poles for such purposes shall be controlled and governed entirely by the ordinances of said city, and all pipes, conduits and poles shall be laid and placed at such points and places as shall be designated by the city engineer and none other, and under the supervision of said city engineer and the supervisor of streets, and to their approval. All excavations made for the erection of poles or the laying of gas or steam mains or conduits shall be repaired by the said grantee, his heirs and assigns, at their own expense to the satisfaction of the city engineer.

Sec. 5. That said S. F. Walker, his heirs and assigns, shall be responsible for any damage to person or property resulting from any act or negligence on their part which may accrue by reason of the exercise of any of the privileges herein granted. Any damage that may be occasioned to any sewer or water pipe by said grantee, his heirs or assigns, in placing any of said poles, conduits or pipes mentioned in this grant, or the repairing of the same, shall be repaired and such pipes restored in as good condition as before being damaged by the said grantee at his own expense.

Sec. 6. The grantee, his heirs and assigns, during the period aforesaid, shall, and by the acceptance of the rights and privileges herein granted, does agree with the said city that he, his heirs or assigns, shall charge for manufactured gas under this franchise a price not exceeding two dollars ($2) per thousand feet, and for natural gas a price not exceeding thirty (30) cents per thousand cubic feet, and for electric light a price not exceeding one (1) cent per hour for each sixteen-candle power lamp, and a proportionate charge for all lamps of increased candle power, and for arc lights of two thousand candle power a price not exceeding ten dollars ($10) per month for twelve o'clock service and fifteen dollars ($15) per month for all night service.

And further: After he or his assigns shall have constructed and put in operation the plant necessary therefor, to furnish for the streets, highways and public places of said city in any desired number electric lights at a price not exceeding ten dollars ($10) per month for each arc light of two thousand candle power for all night service each night in the week, and to furnish the city council chamber, city offices, fire station and public library with the necessary current for light continuously during the life of this franchise free of charge.

Sec. 7. Said city reserves the right as a consideration for the granting of this franchise to levy a special tax in addition to the ordinary property tax upon each pole erected in any street, alley or public ground in said city of such sum per annum as the council may deem reasonable; providing such special tax be uniform upon said grantee, his heirs or assigns, and all other persons or corporations using the streets or alleys of said city in a similar manner or for a similar purpose.

Sec. 8. That nothing in this resolution' shall be construed so as to prevent said city hereafter from changing the manner or place of setting poles or stringing wires, or from requiring said

S. F. Walker, his heirs and assigns, to place all wires or conductors under ground.

Sec. 9. Unless a written acceptance of this franchise with the terms and conditions herein contained is filed with the recorder of said city within twenty (20) days after the date of the passage and approval of this franchise, and unless work shall have been begun within one year after said date, the same is to become null and void.

Sec. 10. This franchise to take effect and be in full force from and after its passage and approval.

Passed by the city council of Salt Lake City, Territory of Utah, December 19, 1893, and referred to the mayor for approval.

[Approved the 22nd day of December, 1893].

ROBERT M. JONES.

A RESOLUTION GRANTING CERTAIN PRIVILEGES AND FRANCHISES TO ROBERT M. JONES, HIS HEIRS AND ASSIGNS

SECTION 1. Be it resolved by the city council of Salt Lake City: That Robert M. Jones, his heirs and assigns, have the authority and consent of the city council, and the permission is hereby granted to him, his heirs and assigns, to use and occupy the streets, lanes, alleys and public places of Salt Lake City, for the purpose of conveying electrical currents, by means of suitable poles and wires above the surface of the ground, or by means of suitable pipes or conduits to be laid below the surface of the ground, for the transmission of electrical currents for furnishing power, light and heat to the inhabitants, property owners, manufacturers and users in said city, for the term of twenty-five (25) years from and after the passage of this resolution.

Sec. 2. That the said Robert M. Jones, his heirs and assigns, during said term be, and hereby are, vested with the right and privilege of entering upon the streets, lanes, alleys and public places of said city for the following purposes:

First.—For the right and privilege of erecting and maintaining in the streets, lanes, alleys and public places of said city poles, and attaching thereto and extending thereon wires and other conductors, for the purpose of transmitting electrical currents within the limits of said city for power, lighting and heating and other purposes to the inhabitants thereof.

Second.—The right and privilege of opening said streets, lanes, alleys and public places for the purpose of laying conduits underground, for the purpose of transmitting electrical currents for power, lighting, heating and other purposes to the inhabitants of said city.

Sec. 3. The said Robert M. Jones shall, at least thirty days prior to the commencement of the erection of poles and wires or the laying of conduits within the limits of Salt Lake City, file with the city engineer a plat showing the streets, lanes, alleys and public places of said city where he proposes to locate lines of poles and wires or conduits, which plat shall be subject to the approval of the city council, and be so approved before any work shall be done in any street in pursuance hereof.

Sec. 4. All streets, lanes, alleys and public places that may be opened by the said Robert M. Jones, his heirs and assigns, for the aforesaid purposes, shall be filled in and put in as good repair as they were prior to the opening of the same, and within a reasonable time, so as not to unnecessarily obstruct the free passage over the streets more than may be necessary. The opening of streets and the erection of poles for such purposes shall be controlled and governed by the ordinances of said city. Any removal of pavement for the erection of poles and wires, or

REVISED ORDINANCES. 45

for the laying of conduits, shall be repaired by the said Robert M. Jones, his heirs and assigns, to the satisfaction of the city engineer and board of public works of said city.

Sec. 5. The said Robert M. Jones, his heirs and assigns, shall have the right to open trenches for the purpose of laying said conduits and for the purpose of maintaining them in good repair, and shall have access to all of such conduits as may be necessary from time to time.

Sec. 6. The said Robert M. Jones, his heirs and assigns, shall be responsible for any damage to person or property resulting from any act of negligence on his or their part, should the same occur by any reason of the exercise of any privilege herein granted. Any damage that may be occasioned to any sewer or water pipe by said Robert M. Jones, his heirs or assigns, in placing any of said pipes or conduits mentioned in this resolution under ground, or in repairing the same, shall be repaired and such pipes restored to as good condition as before being damaged by the said Robert M. Jones, and at his own expense.

Sec. 7. The said Robert M Jones, his heirs and assigns, during the period aforesaid shall, and by his acceptance of the privileges hereby granted, agrees with the said city to furnish electric lights to the citizens of said city, through standard types of incandescent lamps, at a price not to exceed one cent per hour for each sixteen-candle power lamp, and a proportionate charge for lamps of increased candle power, and for arc lights of two thousand candle power, at a price not to exceed ten dollars ($10) per month for twelve o'clock service, and fifteen dollars ($15) for all-night service.

Further: To furnish lighting for the streets, highways and public places, for the city in any desired number, at a price not to exceed ten dollars ($10) per month for each two thousand candle power lamp for all-night service each night in the week.

Further: To supply the city council rooms, city offices and public library with their necessary current for lamps, also the current required for use in lighting the grounds surrounding the city and county building, or such part of the same as would be a charge against the said city, from the time the station starts continuously during the life of the franchise, free of charge.

Sec. 8. That Robert M. Jones, his heirs or assigns, shall not dispose of the privileges granted in this franchise to any competing company or person, nor shall said Robert M. Jones, his heirs or assigns, enter into any combination with any electric light, gas or power company, concerning prices to be charged for furnishing light, heat, power or signals, either to the city or private consumers, otherwise this franchise shall become void.

Sec. 9. Unless a written acceptance of this resolution, with the conditions, restrictions and limitations therein contained, is filed by the said Robert M. Jones, his heirs and assigns, with the city recorder of Salt Lake City, within fifteen days from the date of the approval of this resolution, the franchise hereby granted shall be void and of no effect. That the said Robert M. Jones, in accepting this franchise, agrees to construct the most practical device for con-suming or arresting the smoke in all instances wherein coal is used for fuel by the said Robert M. Jones, his heirs and assigns.

Sec. 10. Said city reserves the right, as a consideration for the granting of this franchise, to levy a special tax, in addition to the ordinary property tax, upon each pole erected in any street, alley or public ground in said city, of such sum per annum as the council may deem reasonable.

Sec. 11. That nothing in this resolution shall be construed so as to prevent said city hereafter from changing the manner or place of setting poles, stringing wires, or from requiring said Robert M. Jones, his heirs and assigns, to place all wires and conductors underground.

Sec. 12. That said Robert M. Jones, his heirs and assigns, to have access to all such main pipes or conduits as may be necessary from time to time, and no such main pipes or conduits shall be laid over or nearer than one foot in the clear from any sewer or water pipe, except in crossing the same All pipes, conduits and poles shall be laid and placed at such points and places as shall be designated by the city engineer, and provided further, that said poles shall be set and the wires suspended thereon under the direction of said council, or some person appointed by it.

Sec. 13. That said Robert M. Jones, his heirs or assigns. shall deliver in the city electrical power equal to one thousand horse power by October 1, 1895.

Sec. 14. That in case Robert M. Jones, his heirs and assigns, shall fail or refuse to carry out any of the conditions of this resolution to be kept and performed by him, and within the time specified, this resolution shall become null and void and of no effect.

Sec. 15. This ordinance shall take effect from and after its publication.

Passed by the city council of Salt Lake City, Territory of Utah, July 25, 1893, and referred to the mayor for approval, and within the time prescribed by law, he having failed to approve or disapprove of the same, the said ordinance became valid and of full affect.

[Amended September 25, 1894.]

SALT LAKE & OGDEN GAS & ELECTRIC LIGHT CO.

A RESOLUTION GRANTING CERTAIN PRIVILEGES AND FRANCHISES TO THE SALT LAKE & OGDEN GAS & ELECTRIC LIGHT COMPANY, THE SUCCESSOR AND ASSIGNEE OF THE SALT LAKE CITY GAS COMPANY AND THE SALT LAKE POWER, LIGHT AND HEATING COMPANY, CORPORATIONS HERETOFORE EXISTING IN THE CITY OF SALT LAKE.

Section 1. Be it resolved by the City Council of Salt Lake City: That the Salt Lake & Ogden Gas & Electric Light Company, a corporation existing under the laws of the Territory of Utah, its successors and assigns, have the authority and conent of the said council, and the permission is hereby granted it to use and occupy the streets, lanes, alleys and public places of Salt Lake City, for the purpose of conveying gas and electrical currents by means of suitable pipes or conduits laid or to be laid below the surface of the ground, or by means of wires or conductors placed above said streets, to be used for electrical lighting, and also pipes to be laid below the surface of the groundfor the conveyance of steam for heating, furnishing power and other purposes, to the inhabitants, property owners and users in said city, for the term of twenty-five years from and after the passage of this resolution

Sec. 2. That said company, its successors and assigns, during said term be and hereby are vested with the right and privilege of entering upon the streets, lanes and alleys of said city for the following purposes:

(a. The opening of said streets, alleys, lanes and public places for the purpose of laying gas mains, electrical conduits, or pipes for steam purposes.

b.) The privilege of erecting and maintaining in the streets, lanes and alleys of said city, poles, and attaching thereto and extending and maintaining thereon wires or conductors for the purpose of transmitting electrical currents within the limits of said city, to the inhabitants thereof.

Sec. 3. The said Salt Lake & Ogden Gas & Electric Light Company shall file with the city engineer a plat showing the streets, lanes, alleys and public places of said city where the said company proposes or may hereafter locate gas pipes and electrical conduits, or pipes for steam purposes; and the said company shall have the right to open trenches for the purpose of laying said mains and conduits and for the purpose of maintaining them in good repair. The said company to have access to all such main gas pipes or conduits as may be necessary from time to time: and no railroad track or other like obstruction shall be laid over said gas mains, conduits or steam pipes, or nearer than one foot in the clear laterally, from the bell joint of such gas mains, electrical conduits or said steam pipes, except in crossing the same.

That the said company shall only lay lateral pipes on sides of streets and shall not in any way or manner interfere with the water pipes or sewer pipes of this city, or any other pipes that have been laid in the streets of said city; and they shall at all times conform to all ordinances passed governing franchises and regulating the same from time to time that are passed by the city council regulating the laying of pipes in this city.

Sec. 4. All streets, lanes, alleys and public places that may be opened by the said company for the aforesaid purposes, shall be filled in and put in as good repair as they were prior to the opening of such trenches, so as not to unnecessarily obstruct the free passage over the streets for a longer time than may be necessary. The use of streets for such purposes shall be controlled and governed by the ordinances of said city, and all pipes, conduits and poles shall be laid and placed at such points and places as shall be designated by the city engineer and none other; and under the supervision of said city engineer and the board of public works, and to their approval.

Sec. 5. The said Salt Lake & Ogden Gas & Electric Light Company, its successors and assigns, shall be responsible for any damage to person or property resulting from any act or negligence on its part which may accrue by reason of the exercise of any of the privileges herein.

Sec. 6. The Salt Lake & Ogden Gas & Electric Light Company, during the period aforesaid, shall and by its acceptance of the privileges hereby granted agrees with the said city to furnish manufactured gas to the citizens of said city at a price not exceed $2.20 per thousand cubic feet; and if water gas is furnished the price shall not exceed $1.50 per thousand cubic feet and if natural gas is furnished the price shall not exceed thirty cents per thousand cubic feet, and that the said city for all public purposes of street lighting, or buildings owned by the city, for all hospitals and public buildings for charitable or religious purposes of any kind shall make a discount, from the aforesaid price, of ten per cent. And the said Salt Lake & Ogden Gas & Electric Light Company agrees to furnish an illuminating gas of not less than eighteen candle power, and incandescent electric of not less than sixteen candle power, the same to be subject from time to time to the inspection of a proper officer appointed by said city council, to determine the quality of said illuminating gas and electric light.

Sec. 7. Unless a written acceptance of this resolution, with the conditions, restrictions and limitations therein contained, is filed by the Salt Lake & Ogden Gas & Electric Light Company with the city recorder of Salt Lake City, within sixty days from the date of the passage thereof, this resolution and the franchise hereby granted shall be void and of no effect.

Sec. 8. And all rights and privileges heretofore granted to the Salt Lake City Gas Company and the Salt Lake Power, Light and Heating Company be relinquished on the acceptance of this franchise.

Sec. 9. Nothing in this resolution shall be so construed as to prevent said city at any time hereafter from changing the manner or place of setting poles, stringing wires, or from requiring said company, its successors or assigns, to place all wires or conductors underground.

Passed by the city council May 19, 1893, title approved, and referred to the mayor for his approval.

Returned to the city council May 20, 1893, with the disapproval of the mayor.

The president then put the question: "Shall the ordinance pass notwithstanding the objection of the mayor thereto?" which was duly carried on roll-call, two-thirds of the council-elect voting therefor.

ROCKY MOUNTAIN BELL TELEPHONE COMPANY.

AN ORDINANCE GRANTING TO THE ROCKY MOUNTAIN BELL TELEPHONE COMPANY THE RIGHT TO CONSTRUCT, OPERATE AND MAINTAIN UNDERGROUND PIPES OR CONDUITS AND WIRES OR OTHER CONDUCTORS AND APPLIANCES FOR THE TRANSMISSION OF ELECTRICITY FOR TELEPHONE AND TELEGRAPH PURPOSES IN SALT LAKE CITY.

SECTION 1. Be it ordained by the city council of Salt Lake City: That the Rocky Mountain Bell Telephone Company, its successors and assigns, are hereby granted the right to construct, operate and maintain, along and across the streets, avenues, alleys, or other public thoroughfares in Salt Lake City, underground pipes or conduits with the necessary manholes and other appurtenances, and to place in such pipes or conduits wires or other conductors and appliances for the transmission of electricity for telephone, telegraph and such other purposes as the city council may hereafter authorize. Also, the right to construct, operate and maintain branch pipes or conduits containing wires or other conductors and appliances for transmitting electricity for the use of its several stations, patrons or subscribers at such points in such manner as may be best adapted to the respective location and requirements.

Sec. 2. All trenching or other excavating and all refilling or other work done by the grantee in any of the streets, avenues, alleys or public thoroughfares, shall be under the supervision and to the satisfaction of the city engineer and board of public works of Salt Lake City, and in case any curb, gutter or pavement or other public property shall be displaced in excavating any work herein authorized, the same shall be restored by the city under the supervision of its engineer and board of public works, and the cost of such restoration shall be paid by the grantee; provided, that before said grantee shall disturb any curb, gutter or pavement or other public improvement, it shall on the request of the city council or board of public works, furnish a bond with good and sufficient sureties to the satisfaction of said council or board of public works, to protect the city from all injury to its property by reason of such disturbance.

Sec. 3. Before commencing on any section or division of the work herein authorized, the grantee, its successors or assigns, shall prepare and file with the city engineer detailed plans of the proposed work on such section or division, showing its location, dimensions and character, and all such plans shall be acceptable to the city engineer and board of public works. And the work shall be performed in strict accordance with the plans so approved, and to the acceptance of the city engineer and board of public works.

Sec. 4. In all of the pipes or conduits constructed under authority of this ordinance, the grantee, its successors or assigns, shall provide all the space necessary for the wires or other conductors of the police and fire departments of the city, for telephone and telegraph purposes, and such space shall be used by the city free of cost or rent during the life of this franchise. The city through its electrical superitendent or other designated agents shall have free access to said pipes or conduits at all times for the purpose of placing, replacing, repairing or removing its wires or other conductors, for which purpose it shall have equal rights with the grantee, its successors and assigns.

Sec. 5. The location of all pipes and conduits shall be such as will not interfere with any sewer, gas or water pipe previously laid, and after the location of said pipes or conduits shall have been fixed in the manner hereinabove provided, the city shall not by subsequent grant or franchise to other parties, permit the same to be interfered with except at the cost of the parties operating under such subsequent franchise, and then only upon condition that any necessary alteration shall be made under direction of the grantee herein, and to such extent only as shall be determined by the city engineer and board of public works; and as shall not permanently impair the franchise hereby granted, or unnecessarily interfere with or injure the structures, operations or business of the said grantee, its successors or assigns.

Sec. 6. Salt Lake City shall in no way be liable or responsible for any action or damage that may occur in the construction or operation of said pipes or conduits, wires or other appliances or appurtenances by reason of the default, or misconduct or otherwise or at all, of the grantee, its successors or assigns, or any of its employees, and the acceptance of this grant shall be deemed on the part of the grantee for itself, its successors and assigns, to save the city harmless from and against all liability, loss, costs, expenses and damages of any nature arising out of any such default or misconduct, or which may accrue by reason of any accident or injury which may occur in or by reason of the construction or operation of said pipes or conduits, wires or other appliances or appurtenances, and to indemnify and repay said city for any loss, costs, expense or damage of any kind it may sustain by reason of any such default, misconduct, accident or injury which may be recovered against said city, the recovery thereof and the judgment therefor shall be final as between the city and the said grantee, its successors and assigns, and conclusive as to the liability of the latter to the former; provided, said grantee shall have notice of the pending of any suit in which such judgment is recovered, and is given an opportunity to defend the same, and provided further, the grantee, its successors and assigns, shall not be liable for any damage for personal or other injuries arising from or growing out of any negligence or want of care on the part of said city, its agents or servants, in its use of said pipes or conduits and appliances or appurtenances.

Sec. 7. Nothing in this ordinance shall be construed as granting to the Rocky Mountain Bell Telephone Company, its successors or assigns, the exclusive right or to prevent the city from granting to other companies or individuals similar rights for like purposes.

Sec. 8. This franchise is granted for a term of thirty-five years from the date of the passage of this ordinance.

Sec 9. If this grant, with all the terms and conditions herein contained, be not accepted in writing by the grantee within sixty days, or if the grantee, its successors or assigns, shall fail to place at least one hundred miles of its wires or other conductors in underground pipes or conduits within one year after the date of its acceptance of this grant, then this franchise shall become null and void, and all of the grantee's rights hereunder shall be forfeited to the city.

Sec. 10. This ordinance shall take effect and be in force from and after its passage.

Passed by the city council of Salt Lake City, Territory of Utah, March 27th, 1894, and referred to the mayor for his approval.

[Approved the 2nd day of April, A. D. 1894.]

HARVEY M. BACON

AN ORDINANCE GRANTING HARVEY M. BACON AND HIS SUCCESSORS AND ASSIGNS A FRANCHISE TO LAY WATER PIPES IN CERTAIN STREETS IN SALT LAKE CITY.

Be it ordained by the council of the city of Salt Lake, Utah:

SECTION 1. That there is hereby granted Harvey M. Bacon, his successors and assigns, for the purpose of erecting and maintaining a bathing resort, or sanitarium, or both, in said city, where the hot mineral waters of the springs in or near the north part of the city may be used, the right to lay and maintain water pipe or pipes, as the city engineer may approve, to conduct such waters along the following mentioned avenues, streets, roads and alleys in said city, to wit: The alleys in the Warm Springs subdivision, Cement avenue, Lime avenue, Agate street, Topaz street, Gem street, County or State road, Second West street, and on Third South street from Second West street into the property now known as the "Palace Stables" on Third South street. Such pipe or pipes to be laid at such place or places in said streets or avenues, roads and alleys as the city engineer may indicate, and under the supervision of the supervisor of streets.

Sec. 2. The pipe or pipes so laid shall be well covered and the trenches kept well filled without expense to the city, and whenever it shall be necessary to open any trench or trenches, for the purpose of making repairs or the laying of pipes or the like, the opening so made shall be properly guarded by said grantee, his successors or assigns, and properly filled so as to make as little obstruction of the streets as possible.

Sec. 3. There is also granted to said grantee, his successors and assigns, the right to lay and maintain a discharge pipe or pipes from the building or buildings to be used as such bath or sanitarium, to the public sewers on Third South street, and discharge the waters of said bath or sanitarium into said sewer, as required by the city ordinances.

If at any time the waters from said bath resort or sanitarium or both, shall have any deleterious effect or in any way damage the sewer pipes of said city, then said grantee, his successors and assigns, within thirty days after being notified of such deleterious effect or damage to such sewer pipes, shall disconnect such discharge pipe or pipes, from said sewer and pay to the city the costs or damages thereof, and may thereafter convey such waste water through a discharge pipe to be laid and maintained by said grantee, his successors and assigns, from said premises to the Jordan river, and said grantee, his successors and assigns, shall have the privilege and are hereby granted the right to lay and maintain a private sewer or discharge pipe in the streets of said city, to carry and discharge said waste waters from said premises into said Jordan river, from the time said grantee, his successors or assigns, shall be required to disconnect their said waste pipe from said city sewer, until the expiration of this franchise. Said waste pipe to be laid under the direction and supervision of the city officer or officers whose duty it shall be to look after and superintend the laying of such pipe or pipes, or such officer or officers as the city council of Salt Lake City shall see fit to appoint for the purpose.

Sec. 4. The franchise herein granted shall continue for a period of twenty-five years from the date of the passage of this ordinance.

Sec. 5. Said city of Salt Lake shall in no way be liable or responsible for accident or damage that may occur by reason of such pipes, or the laying or the maintaining of the same, or by leakage therefrom, or from any sediment, precipitation or injury that may be caused by such water to the sewer pipes of the city, and said grantee, his successors and assigns, covenant and agree to save said city harmless from and against any and all liability, loss, cost, expense or damage arising by reason of said pipes, or the water conveyed thereby, or the maintaining of the same, and to indemnify and repay said city for any loss, cost, expense or damage of any kind which may be sustained by reason of such pipes or water, and if any judgment, or for any loss or injury, shall be recovered against the said city by reason of such pipes or water, the recovery thereof, and the judgment therefor shall be final as between said city and said grantee, his successors and assigns, and conclusive as to the liability of the latter to the former; provided, that the then holders of this franchise shall have timely notice of such suits and opportuninty to defend the same.

Sec. 6. When any of the streets in which said pipes are laid shall be paved, if thereafter the said grantee, his successors or assigns, shall remove or take up the pavement, or any part of it, to lay or repair any of the pipes, said grantee or his successors or assigns, shall replace such pavement to the satisfaction of the Supervisor of streets, each time in as good condition as before taking it up.

Sec. 7. That said grantee, his successors and assigns, be required to put in operation said bath resort or sanitarium within six (6) months from the date of the passage of this ordinance, otherwise this franchise shall become null and void.

Sec. 8. That said grantee, his successors or assigns, shall give to Salt Lake City a good and sufficent bond, in the penal sum of $25,000, that the bath resort or sanitarium shall be in operation within six (6) months.

Sec. 9. This ordinance shall take effect from and after its passage.

Passed by the City Council of Salt Lake City, Territory of Utah, February 24th, 1893, and referred to the mayor for his approval.

[Approved the 2nd day of March, A. D. 1893.]

CHAPTER IX.

DEPOSIT ON APPLICATION FOR FRANCHISE.

AN ORDINANCE REQUIRING A PAYMENT OF $200.00 TO THE TREASURER OF SALT LAKE CITY BY ANY PERSON, PERSONS, COMPANY OR CORPORATION, WHEN APPLYING TO THE CITY COUNCIL FOR A FRANCHISE, EXTENSION OR RENEWAL OF A FRANCHISE.

SECTION 1. Be it ordained by the city council of Salt Lake City, Territory of Utah: That hereafter, whenever any person, persons, company or corporation shall make application to the city council of Salt Lake City for a franchise, extension or renewal of franchise, said person, persons, company or corporation shall furnish said council with nineteen (19) copies of the resolution or ordinance, and pay into the city treasury of said city the sum of $200.00.

Sec. 2. This ordinance to take effect and be in force from and after its approval.

Passed by the city council of Salt Lake City, Territory of Utah, the 13th day of March, 1894, and referred to the mayor for his approval.

[Approved the 16th day of March. A. D. 1894.]

CHAPTER X.

FENCES. HEIGHT OF FENCES.

AN ORDINANCE PRESCRIBING THE HEIGHT OF FENCES WITHIN A DISTANCE OF LESS THAN TEN FEET FROM THE SIDEWALK LINE.

SECTION 1. Be it ordained by the city council of Salt Lake City, Territory of Utah: That it shall be unlawful for any person or persons or any corporation to erect or maintain, within the corporate limits of said city, any fence running parallel with the sidewalk in said city to a greater height than ten feet within a distance of ten feet of the sidewalk. It is hereby made the duty of the chief of police of the city to notify any person or corporation who may have erected or may hereafter erect any fence contrary to the provisions of this ordinance, to remove the same within twenty days after receiving such notice; provided, that the ordinance shall not apply to existing stone walls, and provided further, that all fences now existing or hereafter erected within a distance of ten feet of the outside line of any sidewalk of said city, shall be subject to the inspection and approval of the inspector of buildings of Salt Lake City, and if disapproved or condemned by such inspector, such fence shall be taken down by the owner within ten days after having been notified of such condemnation.

Sec. 2. Any person or corporation violating any of the provisions of this ordinance shall be punished by a fine in any sum not exceeding fifty dollars.

Sec. 3. All ordinances and parts of ordinances in conflict with the provisions of this ordinance are hereby repealed.

This ordinance shall take effect from and after its passage and approval.

Passed by the city council of Salt Lake City, Territory of Utah, October 2nd, 1894, and referred to the mayor for his approval.

[Approved the 4th day of October, A. D. 1894.]

WIRE FENCES,

AN ORDINANCE AMENDING SECTION 7 OF CHAPTER XXVI OF THE REVISED ORDINANCES OF SALT LAKE CITY

See Revised Ordinances, p. 281.

Be it ordained by the City Council of Salt Lake City, Territory of Utah, that section 7 of chapter 26 of the Revised Ordinances of Salt Lake City, Territory of Utah, be amended to read as follows, to wit: It shall be unlawful for any person to hereafter erect or cause to be erected, or to maintain any barbed wire fence along or adjacent to any street, or as a division fence between adjoining lots or parcels of land, either of which is occupied as a place of residence, within the limits of said city and all such fences so erected or maintained, are hereby declared to be a nuisance.

Any person so erecting, causing to be erected or maintaining any such fence, shall be deemed guilty of a misdemeanor, and, on conviction thereof, shall be fined in any sum not exceeding fifty dollars.

This ordinance to take effect and be in force from and after its passage.

Passed by the city council of Salt Lake City, Territory of Utah, September 8th, 1893, and referred to the Mayor for his approval.

[Approved the 11th day of September, 1893.]

CHAPTER XI.

DISPOSAL OF GARBAGE.

AN ORDINANCE AMENDING SECTION 14, CHAPTER XIX, OF THE REVISED ORDINANCES OF SALT LAKE CITY, OF 1892.

See Revised Ordinances, p. 222.

Amend section 14, by striking out the whole section and substituting the following: The removal of ashes and garbage within Garbage district No. 1 and the removal of combustible garbage within Garbage district No. 2, shall be at the expense of the city.

Passed by the city council of Salt Lake City, Territory of Utah, May 1st, 1894, and referred to the mayor for his approval, and he having failed to approve or disapprove within the time required by law, the same became of full force and effect.

CHAPTER XII.

GARNISHMENT.

AN ORDINANCE IN REFERENCE TO GARNISHEE PROCESS AND WAIVING THE LEGAL RIGHTS OF SALT LAKE CITY IN SUCH CASES:

SECTION 1. Be it ordained by the city council of Salt Lake City, Territory of Utah, that said city hereby waives its rights and legal exemption from garnishment process, and does hereby consent to recognize all legal notices of garnishment legally served upon the treasurer of said city.

Sec. 2. That the wages and salaries of employees and officers of Salt Lake City, under its control, may be attached under garnishee process in the same manner and to the same extent as is provided by the general laws of the Territory, and said laws are hereby made applicable to Salt Lake City; provided, that the notice in such cases shall be served upon the city treasurer, and when a garnishment shall have been served upon the city treasurer, he shall answer the same in writing, in the same manner as is required by the general laws of the Territory in such cases made and provided.

Sec. 3. This ordinance shall take effect and be in force from and after its passage and approval.

Passed by the city council of Salt Lake City, Territory of Utah, December 22nd, 1893, and referred to the mayor for his approval, and within the time prescribed by law, five days, he failed to approve or disapprove of the same, the said ordinance became valid and of full force and effect.

CHAPTER XIII.

HACK REGULATIONS.

AN ORDINANCE IN RELATION TO THE DRIVER, OWNER OR OTHER PERSON HAVING IN CHARGE ANY COACH, HACK, CAB OR OTHER VEHICLE IN SALT LAKE CITY, UTAH TERRITORY.

See Revised Ordinances, Chapter 53.

Section 1. Be it ordained by the city council of Salt Lake City, Territory of Utah, that it shall be unlawful for the driver or other person having in charge in Salt Lake City, Territory of Utah, any coach, hack, cab or other vehicle, used for public hire, to be away from his coach, hack, cab or other vehicle, used as aforesaid, more than ten feet, or for such or any person to sit or stand in or about the door steps, entrance or platforms, or in front of, or in the street in front of, any house, hotel, store or other building in said city, or to solicit business at such places, except as provided in ordinances relative thereto, now of record.

Sec. 2. Any person violating this ordinance shall be guilty of a misdemeanor, and upon conviction thereof, shall be fined in any sum not greater than twenty-five dollars, or imprisoned for a period not to exceed ten days in the city jail of Salt Lake City, Utah Territory, or by both such fine and imprisonment.

Sec. 3. This ordinance shall be in force from and after its approval.

64   REVISED ORDINANCES.

See Revised Ordinances, Chapter 53.

Passed by the city council of Salt Lake City, Territory of Utah, September 4th, 1894, and referred to the mayor for his approval.
[Approved the 7th day of September, A. D. 1894.]

RATES.

AN ORDINANCE TO AMEND SECTION II, CHAPTER 53, OF THE REVISED ORDINANCES OF 1892, OF SALT LAKE CITY.

See Revised Ordinances, p. 457.

SECTION 1. Be it ordained by the city council of Salt Lake City, Territory of Utah: That the first paragraph or subdivision of Section 11, of Chapter 53 of the Revised Ordinances of 1892, of Salt Lake City, be and the same is hereby amended by striking out of said paragraph or subdivision the words "twenty-five" and inserting in lieu thereof the word "fifty."

Sec. 2. This ordinance shall take effect and be in force from and after its approval.

Passed by the city council of Salt Lake City, Territory of Utah, March 30th, 1894, and referred to the mayor for his approval.
[Approved the 31st day of March, A. D. 1894.]

CHAPTER XIV.

INSPECTOR OF OILS.

AN ORDINANCE FIXING THE COMPENSATION OF THE INSPECTOR OF COAL OIL, PETROLEUM AND OTHER MINERAL OILS.

SECTION 1. Be it ordained by the city council of Salt Lake City, Territory of Utah: That all inspectors of coal oil, petroleum or other mineral oils, shall be entitled to demand and receive as compensation for his services as inspector, which shall be paid by the party owning the oil inspected, the following fees, to-wit: For all oils in barrels or tank-cars, one quarter of a cent per gallon. For oils in cases one cent per gallon for lots from one gallon to twenty five gallons; three-fourths of a cent per gallon for all lots from twenty-five gallons to fifty gallons; one-half of a cent per gallon for all lots over fifty gallons. All fees in excess of $900.00 per year shall pe covered into the city treasury.

Sec. 2. This ordinance shall be in force from and after its approval.

Passed by the city council of Salt Lake City, Territory of Utah, June 5th, 1894, and referred to the mayor for his approval.

[Approved the 9th day of June, A. D. 1894.]

CHAPTER XV.

INSPECTION OF LIVE STOCK.

AN ORDINANCE DESIGNATING THE PLACES AND TIME FOR THE INSPECTION OF LIVE STOCK AS TO HEALTH AND OWNERSHIP AS REQUIRED BY AN ACT OF THE TERRITORIAL LEGISLATURE APPROVED MARCH 8TH, 1894.

SECTION 1. Be it ordained by the city council of Salt Lake City, Territory of Utah: That the Union Stock Yards, situated at the southern part of Davis county, and adjoining the north boundary line of said city, and what is known as the Jordan Stock Farm, situated south of said city, and at or near Second West and Twelfth South streets, be, and the same are hereby designated as the places for the inspection, as provided in an act of the territorial legislature approved March 8th, 1894, of all cattle, sheep and swine which are intended for immediate slaughter and consumption for food in said city; and all persons intending to slaughter any such animals, the carcasses of which are to be sold as food in said city, shall take the same to one of said places before mentioned for inspection on the hoof before the same shall be slaughtered.

Sec. 2. The following is hereby designated and adopted as the form of the meat inspection tag to be used by said city, and shall be attached to all carcasses and meats which shall pass an inspection by the city meat inspector, to wit:

Which tag shall be attached to the same by the use of a wire and seal, by the city inspector.

Sec. 3. The rules, regulations and method of inspection adopted by the Bureau of Animal Industry conducted by the United States government, shall be taken as the standard of meat inspection by said city, and shall be followed as closely as may be practicable.

Sec. 4. The inspection on the hoof shall be made on each day in the week if necessary, Sundays excepted, at the Union Stock Yards between the hours of 9 a. m. and 12 m., and at the Jordan Stock Farm between the hours of 2 p. m. and 6 p. m.

Sec. 5. The said inspector shall receive a salary for his services of $100.00 per month.

Sec. 6. This ordinance shall take effect and be in force from and after its approval.

Passed by the city council of Salt Lake City, Territory of Utah, June 5th, 1894, and referred to the mayor for his approval.

[Approved the 9th day of June, A. D. 1894.]

CHAPTER XVI.

BUTCHERS' LICENSE.

AN ORDINANCE TO REGULATE, LICENSE, RESTRAIN AND PROHIBIT SLAUGHTERERS, BUTCHERS AND DEALERS IN FRESH MEATS

SECTION 1. Be it and it is hereby ordained by the city council of Salt Lake City, Territory of Utah: That every person, firm or corporation before engaging in the business of slaughtering, butchering, selling, handling, bartering or exchanging fresh meats within this city must obtain a license therefor and make yearly payments into the city treasury in advance as follows:

For slaughterers or butchers (who are not vendors) . . . $ 25 00
For all wholesale or commission merchants handling fresh
 meats, whose sales amount to $10,000 or less per month 100 00
For sales over $10,000 and less than $20,000 per month . 150 00
For sales over $20,000 and less than $30,000 per month . . 200 00
For sales over $30,000 per month 250 00
For all retail dealers and traffickers in fresh meats whose
 sales amount to $500 or less per month 50 00
For sales over $500 and less than $1,000 per month . . . 75 00
For sales over $1,000 and less than $2,500 per month . 100 00
For sales over $2,500 and less than $5,000 per month . . 125 00
For sales over $5,000 per month 150 00

Sec. 2. Before any such license is issued there shall be filed with the city treasurer an application on oath, which shall show the name of the applicant, the street and number of his place of business, the average amount of sales made per month during the next preceding year, providing said business has been transacted during said time, and if not an estimate from the best information to be obtained of the average monthly sales to be made.

Sec. 3. Within the limits of Salt Lake City, no license shall be granted to peddle or hawk upon or along any of the streets thereof any fresh meats, beef, veal, lamb or mutton; and any person or persons who shall sell or dispose of any fresh meats, beef, veal, lamb or mutton within said city, except as in this ordinance provided, shall be subject to the fine hereinafter provided.

Provided, however, that the provisions of this ordinance shall not be construed to prevent a farmer from disposing of the meat product of his own raising, if not engaged in the business of selling meats.

Sec. 4. None of the licenses herein mentioned shall be issued for a period of less than one year.

Sec. 5. Any person violating any of the provisions of this ordinance shall upon conviction be fined in any sum not exceeding two hundred dollars.

Sec. 6. So much of the ordinances of this city heretofore existing as conflict with the foregoing sections of this ordinance are hereby repealed.

Sec. 7. This ordinance shall take effect and be in force from and after its passage.

Passed by the city council of Salt Lake City, Utah Territory, August the 2nd, 1894, and referred to the mayor for his approval.

[Approved the 6th day of August, A. D. 1894.]

CHAPTER XVII.

MILK LICENSE.

AN ORDINANCE AMENDING SECTIONS 8, 10 AND 13, OF CHAPTER 18 OF THE REVISED ORDINANCES OF SALT LAKE CITY, OF 1892.

Be it ordained by the city council of Salt Lake City, Territory of Utah: That Section 13 of Chapter 18, of the Revised Ordinances of Salt Lake City, of 1892, be amended to read as follows:

I. No person shall bring or send into said city for sale or offer for sale or sell in said city any milk without having first obtained from the board of health of said city a permit so to do. Such permit shall be given by said board of health whenever upon inspection of the premises where the cows are kept and inspection of the vessels used to hold such milk, and test of the milk, it shall appear that said premises and vessels are kept in good sanitary condition, and that the milk meets the requirements of the ordinances and the rules adopted by such board of health, and upon condition that none but pure, unadulterated and undiluted milk shall be sold and that yearly license shall be paid as follows:

See Revised Ordinances, pp. 217-18.

On daily sales of not more than two gallons, $1.00; on daily sales of two gallons and not more than five gallons, $3.00; on each additional five gallons or part thereof sold daily, $2.50.

II. After such permit shall have been granted, the inspector of provisions of said city shall have power to condemn milk whenever upon inspection of premises and vessels and test of milk, it shall be found that such premises or vessels are not kept in good sanitary condition or that the milk does not meet the requirements of the ordinances and the rules adopted by said board of health; and it shall be unlawful for any person to sell or offer for sale any milk so condemned.

See Revised Ordinances, pp. 217-18.

Amend section 8 by adding the words "or brewer's malt" after word "swill."

Amend section 10 by adding the words "sanitary condition" after the word "ventilation."

This ordinance shall be in effect from and after its approval.

Passed by the city council of Salt Lake City, Territory of Utah, August 7th, 1894, and referred to the mayor for his approval.

[Approved the 11th day of August, A. D., 1894.

CHAPTER XVIII.

PAYROLLS.

AN ORDINANCE REQUIRING THE HEADS OF DEPARTMENTS TO VERIFY STATEMENTS AND PAYROLLS.

Section 1. Be it ordained by the city council of Salt Lake City: That the chief or head of each department shall hereafter verify under oath all payrolls and statements involving the payment of money, as to the correctness of such payrolls or statements, and that no payroll or statement shall be accepted, acted upon or approved until verified as above provided.

Sec. 2. This ordinance shall take effect from and after its passage.

Passed by the city council of Salt Lake City, Territory of Utah, June 20, 1893, and referred to the mayor for his approval.

[Approved by the mayor June 23, 1893.]

CHAPTER XIX.

PAVING DISTRICTS.

AN ORDINANCE CREATING, DEFINING AND ESTABLISHING PAVING DISTRICTS NOS. 10, 11, 12 AND 13, IN SALT LAKE CITY.

SECTION 1. Be it ordained by the city council of Salt Lake City, Territory of Utah: That the following paving districts are hereby created and established in Salt Lake City, as follows, to-wit:

District No. 10.

District No. 10 shall be and consist of all that portion of State street of said city, being and lying between the north line of Fourth South street, and the north line of Eighth South street of said city.

District No. 11.

District No. 11 shall be and consist of all that portion of South Temple street of said city, being and lying between the east line of West Temple street and the east line of Fourth West street of said city.

District No. 12.

District No. 12 shall be and consist of all that portion of First South street from the east line of First West street to the east line of Fifth West street of said city.

District No. 13.

District No. 13 shall be and consist of all that portion of Second South street from the east line of First West street to the east line of Sixth West street of said city.

All the above named streets and parts of streets lying and being within the corporate limits of Salt Lake City, Territory of Utah.

Sec. 2. This ordinance shall be in force from and after its approval.

Passed by the city council of Salt Lake City, Territory of Utah, April 11th, 1893, and referred to the mayor for his approval.

[Approved by the mayor April 14th, 1893.]

CHAPTER XX.

POLICE.

CHIEF—EX-OFFICIO JAILOR.

AN ORDINANCE AUTHORIZING THE CHIEF OF POLICE TO ACT AS EX-OFFICIO JAILOR.

Be it ordained by the city council of Salt Lake City, Territory of Utah:

Section 1. That the chief of police shall be, and he is hereby made, ex-officio jailor, and as such shall perform all of the duties to that office, and may, with the approval of the mayor, by and with the advice and consent of the city council, appoint an assistant jailor, for whose acts he shall be responsible.

Sec. 2. The chief of police shall not receive any compensation, other than his regular salary, for his services as jailor, but the salary of the assistant jailor shall be one thousand and twenty dollars ($1,020) per year.

Sec. 3. This ordinance to take effect and be in force from and after its passage and approval, and all provisions of ordinances in conflict with the foregoing are hereby repealed.

Passed by the city council of Salt Lake City, Territory of Utah, January 30th, 1894, and referred to the mayor for his approval.

[Approved the 5th day of February, 1894.]

NUMBER OF FORCE.

AN ORDINANCE FIXING THE NUMBER OF THE REGULAR POLICE FORCE IN SALT LAKE CITY.

SECTION 1. Be it ordained by the city council of Salt Lake City, Territory of Utah, that the regular police force of Salt Lake City be and the same is hereby fixed at not to exceed forty-one men, including the captain.

All ordinances or parts of ordinances or resolutions in conflict herewith are hereby repealed.

Sec. 2. This ordinance shall be in force from and after its approval.

Passed by the city council of Salt Lake City, Territory of Utah, August 14, 1894, and referred to the mayor for his approval; and, within the time prescribed by law, he having failed to approve or disapprove, the same became valid and of full effect.

DETECTIVE.

AN ORDINANCE AUTHORIZING THE MAYOR TO APPOINT A SPECIAL POLICEMAN FOR A LONGER PERIOD THAN TEN DAYS, TO BE DETAILED FOR DETECTIVE WORK.

Be it ordained by the city council of Salt Lake City, Territory of Utah: That the mayor of Salt Lake City is hereby authorized and empowered to appoint a special policeman to be by him detailed for detective work who shall hold his office during the pleasure of the mayor or until further order of the city council: said special policeman shall receive a salary of $90 per month.

This ordinance to take effect and be in force from and after its passage and approval.

Passed by the city council of Salt Lake City, Territory of Utah, February 2nd, 1894. and referred to the mayor for his approval.

[Approved the 7th day of February. A. D. 1894.]

CHAPTER XXI.

STREETS.

FIRES IN STREETS.

AN ORDINANCE PROHIBITING THE BUILDING OF FIRES ON STREETS PAVED WITH ASPHALT OR OTHER MATERIAL OF A SIMILAR NATURE IN SALT LAKE CITY

SECTION 1. Be it ordained by the city council of Salt Lake City, Salt Lake County, Territory of Utah: That it is unlawful for any person or persons to build, maintain, or to assist in maintaining any bonfire or any fire upon any of the streets within the corporate limits of Salt Lake City, paved with asphalt or other material of a similar nature.

Sec. 2. Any person violating any of the provisions of this ordinance shall, on conviction, be fined in any sum less than fifty dollars.

Sec. 3. This ordinance shall take effect and be in force from and after its approval.

Passed by the city council of Salt Lake City, Utah Territory, December 9th, 1892, and referred to the mayor for his approval.
[Approved the 13th day of December, A. D. 1892.]

WEST CAPITOL STREET.

AN ORDINANCE CHANGING THE NAME OF GREEN STREET IN SALT LAKE CITY.

SECTION 1. Be it ordained by the city council of Salt Lake City, Territory of Utah: That Section 18 of Chapter 46, of the Revised Ordinances of Salt Lake City, of 1892, be and the same is hereby amended as follows, to-wit: Strike out the word "Green" in the third line from the bottom of said section 18 and insert the words "West Capitol" in lieu thereof.

Sec. 2. This ordinance shall be in force from and after its approval.

Passed by the city council of Salt Lake City, Territory of Utah, December 23rd, 1893, and referred to the mayor for his approval, and within the time prescribed by law, he having failed to approve or disapprove of the same, the said ordinance became valid and of full effect.

See Revised Ordinances, p. 417

EXCAVATIONS.

AN ORDINANCE AMENDING CHAPTER 6 OF THE COMPILED ORDINANCES OF SALT LAKE CITY, BY STRIKING OUT SECTION 9 OF SAID CHAPTER AND ADOPTING THE FOLLOWING IN LIEU THEREOF.

SECTION 1. Be it ordained by the city council of Salt Lake City, Territory of Utah: That section 9 of chapter 6 of the Compiled Ordinances of Salt Lake

See Revised Ordinances p. 42

City be and the same is hereby repealed, and the following adopted as section 9 in lieu thereof: Section 9. It shall be the duty of all contractors, corporations or persons, who shall make any excavation in any of the streets, avenues or alleys in Salt Lake City; or who shall obstruct any of said streets, alleys or avenues in any manner, or perform any work therein: to erect and maintain proper guards, signals, barricades and lights at all such places: to replace all earth, paving or other material removed from any of the streets, avenues or alleys, in a proper manner: and that all earth so removed be solidly stamped where replaced, and left in as safe and good condition as it was before the same was removed; and be by them maintained in such condition for six months: that when paving material is removed, that the same is kept properly separated from the soil, and that the same shall be replaced in as good and substantial condition as before such removal, and that all deficiencies in such paving are made good when the paving is replaced: that all surplus material shall be taken off the street by such person, contractor or corporation; and said street, avenue or alley placed in a good and safe condition for the use of the public, immediately upon the completion of the work on said street, avenue or alley. That any contractor, corporation or person failing, neglecting or refusing to comply with any of the provisions of this section shall, on conviction, be subject to a fine in any sum not less than twenty-five dollars ($25), nor more than one hundred dollars ($100), and shall pay all damages which may be sustained by any person by reason of a failure to comply with any of the provisions of this section; any judgment obtained against said city by reason of the neglect, failure or refusal on the part of any contractor, corporation or

See Revised Ordinances, p. 142.

person, together with the costs taxed against said city in the case together with 10 per cent. interest per annum upon the amount of said judgment and costs, shall be the manner of damages in any suit between the city and such corporation, contractor or person, for any such neglect, failure or refusal.

See Revised Ordinances, p. 142.

Sec. 2. This ordinance shall take effect and be in force from and after its approval.

Passed by the city council of Salt Lake City, Territory of Utah, April 7th, 1893, and referred to the mayor for his approval.

[Approved the 12th day of April, 1893.]

REPAIR OF PAVEMENTS.

AN ORDINANCE AMENDING SECTION 10, OF CHAPTER 6, OF THE REVISED ORDINANCES OF SALT LAKE CITY.

SECTION 1. Be it ordained by the city council of Salt Lake City, Territory of Utah: That section 10, of chapter 6, of the revised ordinances of 1892 be amended by adding at the end of said section the following, to-wit:

"That before any permit shall be granted by the board of public works or be issued by the chairman thereof, authorizing any person to make an excavation in any street, sidewalk, alley or other public place or to remove any pavement, curb, gutter or other material or improvement thereon, the chairman of said board shall make an estimate of the probable cost of replacing the material to be excavated or removed and of restoring the street, sidewalk, alley or other public place to the same condition it was in previous to making the excavation or removing the materials or improvements contemplated in such permit; and require the applicant

See Revised Ordinances, p. 142.

therefor to deposit the amount of such estimated cost with the board of public works to be used by said board in paying to replace the materials excavated or removed by said applicant and to restore the street, sidewalk, alley or other public place to its former condition; and that after the cost of such restoration shall have been paid by the board out of said deposit, the remainder thereof, if any, shall be returned by said board to the depositor."

See Revised Ordinances, p. 142.

Sec. 2. This ordinance shall take effect and be in force from and after its approval.

Passed by the city council of Salt Lake City, Territory of Utah, August 7th, 1894, and referred to the mayor for his approval.

[Approved the 11th day of August, A. D., 1894.

CHAPTER XXII.

SPRINKLING DISTRICTS.

NUMBER THREE.

AN ORDINANCE CREATING AND DEFINING THE BOUNDARIES OF SPRINKLING DISTRICT NO. 3 IN SALT LAKE CITY.

SECTION 1. Be it ordained by the city council of Salt Lake City, County of Salt Lake, Territory of Utah:

That the following Sprinkling District No 3 is hereby created, defined, bounded and established in Salt Lake City, to wit: All of Fifth South street, from Ninth East street east to Mount Olivet cemetery; all of Sixth South street from Seventh East street to Thirteenth East street; all of Sixth South street, from Second West street to Fourth West street; all of Tenth East street, from Fourth South street to Fifth South street; all of Thirteenth East street, from Fifth South street to Sixth South street; all of Eleventh East street, from Fifth South street to Seventh South street; and all of Second North street, from Second West street to Third West street; all of Ninth East between Sixth and Seventh South, and Seventh South between Seventh and Ninth East, Sixth South between Sixth and Seventh East, and Sixth South between First and Second West. That all of the aforesaid mentioned streets and territory shall be known as Sprinkling District No. 3.

Sec. 2. This ordinance shall take effect and be in force from and after its approval.

Passed by the city council of Salt Lake City, Territory of Utah, May 23rd, 1893, and referred to the mayor for his approval.

[Approved by the mayor May 27, 1893.]

NUMBER FOUR.

AN ORDINANCE CREATING SPRINKLING DISTRICT TO BE DESIGNATED AS SPRINKLING DISTRICT NO. 4 AND DEFINING THE BOUNDARIES THEREOF.

SECTION 1. Be it ordained by the city council of Salt Lake City, Territory of Utah: That Sprinkling District No. 4, of Salt Lake City, is hereby created and established and its boundaries and arae of streets, and territory included in said district, described as follows to-wit:

All of Third West street from South Temple to Second North street. All of First North street from Second West street to Third West streets. All of North Temple street from Second West to Third West streets. All of Fourth South street from Second West street to Fourth West street. All of Third West street from Third South street to Fourth South street. All of Third West street from First South street to Second South street. That an ordinance heretofore passed creating and defining the boundaries of Sprinkling District No. 2, so far as the same is in conflict with this ordinance, be and the same is hereby repealed.

Sec. 2. This ordinance shall take effect and be in force from and after its approval.

Passed by the city council of Salt Lake City, Territory of Utah, this the 27th day of April, A. D. 1894, and referred to the mayor for his approval.

[Approved the 28th day of April, A. D. 1894.]

NUMBER FIVE.

AN ORDINANCE CREATING SPRINKLING DISTRICT NO 5 AND DEFINING THE BOUNDARIES THEREOF.

Section 1. Be it ordained by the city council of Salt Lake City, Territory of Utah:

That Sprinkling District No. 5 of Salt Lake City be and the same is hereby created and established, and its boundaries and area of streets, and territory included in said district is described as follows, to wit: Commencing at east side of State street on the north side of South Temple street, running thence east to the east line of S street, thence north on the east line of S street to the north line of First street, thence west along the north line of First street to the east line of R street, thence north along the east line of R street to the north line of Second street, thence west along the north line of Second street, to the east line of Q street, thence north along the east line of Q street to the north line of Fourth street, thence west along the north line of Fourth street to the west line of B street, thence south along the west line of B street to the north line of Third street, thence west along the north line of Third street to the west line of A street, thence south along the west line of A street to the north line of First street, thence west along the north line of First street to the east line of State street, thence north along the east line of State street to the north line of North Temple street, thence west across State street to the west line of State street, thence south along the west line of State street to the north line of South Temple street, thence east along the north line of South Temple street to the place of beginning. All of Canyon road from State street to Fourth street

That all ordinances and parts of ordinances in conflict with this ordinance are hereby repealed.

Sec. 2. This ordinance shall take effect and be in force from and after its approval.

Passed by the city council of Salt Lake City, Utah Territory, this the 27th day of April, A.D. 1894, and referred to the mayor for his approval.

[Approved the 28th day of April, A. D. 1894.]

NUMBER SIX.

AN ORDINANCE CREATING AND DEFINING SPRINKLING DISTRICT NO. 6, IN SALT LAKE CITY

SECTION 1. Be it ordained by the city council of Salt Lake City, Territory of Utah:

That Sprinkling District No. 6 of Salt Lake City, Territory of Utah, is hereby created and its area of streets defined as follows: All of Second, Third and Fourth East streets, between Seventh and Ninth South streets; all of Seventh and Eighth East streets, between Fifth and Ninth South streets; all of Ninth East street, between Fifth and Sixth South streets; all of Ninth East street, between Seventh and Ninth South streets; all of Tenth East street, between Fifth and Ninth South streets; all of Seventh South street, between First and Fifth East streets; all of Seventh South street, between Sixth and Seventh East streets; all of Seventh South street, between Ninth and Tenth East streets; all of Eighth South street, between State and Fifth East streets; all of Eighth South street, between First and Fifth East streets; all of Eighth South street, between Sixth and Tenth East streets; all of Ninth South street, between State and Tenth East streets; all of First West street, between Seventh and Ninth South streets; all of Second West street, between Fifth and Ninth South streets; all of Third West street, between Second and Third South streets; all of Third West street, between Fourth and Ninth South streets; all of Fourth West street, between First North and Ninth South streets; all of Fifth West street, between First North and Ninth South streets; all of South Temple street, between Third West and Fifth West streets; all of First South street, between Fourth West and Fifth West streets; all of Fourth South street, between Fourth West and Fifth West streets; all of Fifth South street, between Second West and Fifth West streets; all of Sixth South street, between Fourth West and Fifth West streets; all of Seventh South street, between West Temple and Fifth West streets; all of Eighth South street, between West Temple and Fifth West streets; all of Ninth South street, between West Temple and Fifth West streets; all of Washington street, between Eighth and Ninth South streets; all of Jefferson street, between Eighth and Ninth South streets; all of Blair avenue, between Eighth and Ninth South streets; all of Lincoln avenue, between Eighth and Ninth South streets; all of Green avenue, between Eighth and Ninth South streets; all of First North street, between Third and Fifth West streets; all of North Temple street, between Third and Fifth West streets; all of First North street, between First East or State street and West Temple street; and all of First East or State street, between North Temple and First North streets.

Sec. 2. This ordinance shall take effect and be in force from and after its approval.

Passed by the city council of Salt Lake City, Territory of Utah, June 5th, 1894, and referred to the mayor for his approval.

[Approved the 9th day of June, A. D. 1894.]

CHAPTER XXIII.

SEWER DISTRICTS.

NUMBERS ONE AND TWO.

AN ORDINANCE CREATING AND ESTABLISHING SEWER DISTRICTS NUMBERED 1 AND 2; DEFINING THEIR BOUNDARIES, AND REPEALING ALL ORDINANCES NOW IN FORCE IN CONFLICT HEREWITH.

See Revised Ordinances, pp. 372-74.

SECTION 1. Be it ordained by the city council of Salt Lake City, Territory of Utah:

That sewer districts numbered 1 and 2 are hereby created and established, with the following boundaries, to wit: Boundaries of sewer district No. 1—Beginning for the same at a point where the north line of the southeast quarter of section 23, township 1 north, range 1 west, Salt Lake meridian, intersects the center line of the county road; then southeasterly along the center of the county road to the intersection of the center line of Garnet street in the "Warm Springs subdivision;" thence south to the center of block 170, plat A; thence east to the intersection of the center line of Third West street; thence south to the stone monument at the intersection of Eighth North and

Third West streets; thence east to a point opposite the center of block 156, plat A; thence south through the center of said block 156 to the center of block 151, plat A; thence east to the intersection of the center line of Second West street; thence south to the stone monument at the intersection of Sixth North and Second West streets; thence east to a point opposite the center of block 139, plat A; thence south through blocks 139 and 132 to the center of block 121, plat A; thence west to the center of block 120, plat A; thence south to the center of block 115, plat A; thence west to the intersection of the center line of Third West street; thence south to the stone monument at the intersection of Second North and Third West streets; thence west to a point opposite to the center of block 101, plat A; thence south through the center of said block 101 to the center of block 98, plat A; thence west to the intersection of the center line of Fourth West street; thence south to the stone monument at the intersection of Fourth West and South Temple streets; thence east to a point opposite the center of block 80, plat A; thence south through the center of said block 80 to the center of block 65, plat A; thence east to the intersection of the center line of Third West street; thence south to the stone monument at the intersection of Second South and Third West streets; thence east to a point opposite the center of block 61, plat A; thence south to the center of said block 61; thence east to the intersection of the center line of Second West street; thence south to the stone monument at the intersection of Third South and Second West streets; thence east to a point opposite the center of block 49, plat A; thence south to the center of said block 49; thence east to the intersection of the center line of First West street; thence south to the stone monument at the intersec-

See Revised Ordinances, pp. 372-74.

tion of Fourth South and First West streets; thence east to a point opposite the center of block 41, plat A: thence south to the center of said block 41; thence east through blocks 41, 40 and 39 to the intersection of the center line of State street; thence south to the stone monument at the intersection of State and Fifth South streets; thence east to a point opposite the center of block 35, plat A; thence south to the center of said block 35; thence east to the center of block 36, plat A; thence south to the center of block 19, plat A; thence east to the center of block 21, plat B; thence south to the intersection of the center line of Seventh South street; thence east to the stone monument at the intersection of Fourth East and Seventh South streets; thence south to a point opposite the center of block 9, plat B: thence east to the center of said block 9; thence south to the center of block 6, plat B; thence east to the intersection of the center line of Fifth East street; thence south to the intersection of the center line of Eleventh South street; thence east along the center of Eleventh South street to the intersection of the center line of Ninth East street; thence south along the center of Ninth East street to a point opposite the southwest corner of lot 8, block 1, five-acre plat A; thence east along the south boundary line of the city to the east line of Fifteenth East street; thence north along the east side of Fifteenth east street to the boundary line of the Fort Douglas military reservation; thence west to the brick monument at the southwest corner of the said reservation; thence north along the west boundary of the said reservation to the south line of the southwest quarter of section 28, township 1 north, range 1 east of the Salt Lake meridian; thence west to the southwest corner of section 29, township 1 north, range 1 east; thence north 80 rods; thence west 400

See Revised Ordinances, pp. 372-74.

rods; thence north 80 rods; thence west 80 rods to the center of section 25, township 1 north, range 1 west; thence north 160 rods to the southeast corner of the southwest quarter of section 24, township 1 north, range 1 west; thence west 80 rods; thence north 80 rods; thence west 80 rods; thence north 80 rods to the quarter-section corner between sections 23 and 24, township 1 north, range 1 west; thence west to place of beginning.

Boundaries of Sewer District No. 2—Beginning at point where the north line of the southeast quarter of section 22, township 1 north, range 1 west, intersects the east bank of the Jordan river, and running thence east to a point where the north boundary line of the southeast quarter of section 23, township 1 north, range 1 west, intersects the center line of the county road; thence southeasterly along the center of the county road to the intersection of the center line on Garnet street, in the Warm Springs subdivision; thence south to the center of block 170, plat A; thence east to the intersection of the center line of Third West street; thence south to the stone monument at the intersection of Eighth North and Third West streets; thence east to a point opposite the center of block 156, plat A; thence south through the center of said block 156 to the center of block 151, plat A; thence east to the intersection of the center line of Second West street; thence south to the stone monument at the intersection of Sixth North and Second West streets; thence east to a point opposite the center of block 139, plat A; thence south through blocks 139 and 132 to the center of block 121, plat A; thence west to the center of block 120, plat A; thence south to the center of block 115, plat A; thence west to the intersection of the center line of Third West street; thence south to the stone monument at the intersection of Second North and Third West

See Revised Ordinances, pp. 372-74.

streets; thence west to a point opposite the center of block 101, plat A; thence south through the center of said block 101 to the center of block 98, plat A; thence west to the intersection of the center line of Fourth West street; thence south to the stone monument at the intersection of Fourth West and South Temple streets; thence east to a point opposite the center of block 80, plat A; thence south through the center of said block 80 to the center of block 65, plat A; thence east to the intersection of the center line of Third West street; thence south to the stone monument at the intersection of Second South and Third West streets; thence east to a point opposite the center of block 61, plat A; thence south to the center of said block 61; thence east to the intersection of the center line of Second West street; thence south to the stone monument at the intersection of Third South and Second West streets; thence east to a point opposite the center of block 49, plat A; thence south to the center of said block 49; thence east to the intersection of the center line of First West street; thence south to the stone monument at the intersection of Fourth South and First West streets; thence east to a point opposite the center of block 41, plat A; thence south to the center of said block 41; thence east through blocks 41, 40 and 39 to the intersection of the center line of State street; thence south to the stone monument at the intersection of State and Fifth South streets; thence east to a point opposite the center of block 35, plat A; thence south to the center of said block 35; thence east to the center of block 36, plat A; thence south to the center of block 19, plat A; thence east to the center of block 21, plat B; thence south to the intersection of the center line of Seventh South street; thence east to the stone monument at the inter-

See Revised Ordinances, pp. 372-74.

section of Fourth East and Seventh South streets; thence south to a point opposite the center of block 9, plat B; thence east to the center of the said block 9; thence south to the center of block 6, plat B; thence east to the intersection of the center line of Fifth East street; thence south to the south line of Tenth South or Roper street; thence west along the south line of Tenth South or Roper street to the east bank of the Jordan river; thence down the east bank of the Jordan river to the place of beginning.

Sec. 2. All ordinances and parts of ordinances in conflict with this ordinance are hereby repealed.

Sec. 3. This ordinance shall take effect and be in force from and after its approval.

Passed by the city council of Salt Lake City, Territory of Utah, September 1, 1893, and referred to the mayor for his approval.

The mayor failed to approve or disapprove the same within five days, the period prescribed by law, and by virtue thereof the ordinance becomes in full force and effect.

See Revised Ordinances, pp. 372-74.

CHAPTER XXIV.

SALOONS.

BOYS IN SALOONS.

AN ORDINANCE MAKING IT UNLAWFUL FOR PERSONS UNDER THE AGE OF EIGHTEEN YEARS TO VISIT, FREQUENT OR PLAY BILLIARDS OR POOL, OR BE PERMITTED TO VISIT, FREQUENT OR PLAY BILLIARDS OR POOL IN ANY SALOON OR PLACE WHERE INTOXICATING LIQUORS ARE SOLD

SECTION 1. Be it ordained by the city council of Salt Lake City, Territory of Utah:

That it shall be unlawful for any person or persons who keep a saloon or other place where intoxicating liquors are sold to permit any person under the age of eighteen years to visit, frequent or remain in such saloon or place, or to play billiards or pool therein, or in any room or hall connecting with or adjoining to such saloon or place.

Any person violating any of the provisions of this section, on conviction therefor, shall be punished by fine in any sum not exceeding one hundred dollars ($100), or by imprisonment not exceeding forty days, or by both fine and imprisonment, in the discretion of the court.

Sec. 2. It shall be unlawful for any person under the age of eighteen years to visit, frequent or remain in any saloon or place where intoxicating liquor is sold; or to visit, frequent, remain in, or play billiards or pool in any such saloon or place, or in any room or hall connected with or adjoining to such saloon or place.

Any boy violating any of the provisions of this section, upon conviction thereof, shall be punished by a fine in any sum not exceeding twenty-five dollars ($25), or by imprisonment not exceeding ten days, or by both fine and imprisonment, in the discretion of the court.

Sec. 2. This ordinance shall take effect and be in force from and after its approval.

Passed by the city council of Salt Lake City, Territory of Utah, March 28, 1893, and referred to the mayor for his approval.

[Approved by the mayor March 31, 1893.]

CHAPTER XXV.

SALARIES.

OFFICERS AND EMPLOYEES.

AN ORDINANCE FIXING THE SALARIES AND COMPENSATION OF CERTAIN OFFICERS AND EMPLOYEES OF SALT LAKE CITY.

SECTION 1. Be it ordained by the city council of Salt Lake City, Territory of Utah:

That the salaries and compensation of the following named officers and employees of said city be and the same are hereby fixed as follows, for the term of office to which each of them may have been elected or appointed, to wit:

Assessor and collector of water rates, $1,200 per year.

See Revised Ordinances, p. 362.

Deputy assessor and collector of water rates, $900 per year.

City attorney, $2,500 per year.

Assistant city attorney, $1,000 per year.

Auditor's deputy, $1,200 per year.

Board of Health—

Clerk of board of health, $900 per year.

That the office of city physician be and the same is hereby abolished.

Health commissioner, who shall also perform the duties heretofore performed by the city physician, $1,500 per year.

Board of Public Works—
Chairman board of public works, $1,500 per year.
Each member of the board, other than the chairman, $200 per year.
Clerk of the board, $720 per year.

Fire Department—
Chief of fire department, $1,800 per year.
Assistant chief, $1,296 per year.
Engineers of steamers, $1,140 per year.
Captains, each, $1,080 per year.
Secretary, $1,080 per year.
Drivers, each, $960 per year.
Tillermen, each, $960 per year.
Relief drivers, pipemen, laddermen and stokers, each, $960 per year.
Callmen, for each day of actual service, $2.50 per day.

See Revised Ordinances, p. 362.

Police Department—
Duty sergeants, each, $1,200 per year.
Mounted police, each, $1,200 per year.
Patrolmen, first year, $1,020 per year.
Patrolmen, second year, $1,080 per year.
Special policemen, $2.50 per day.
Liberty park policeman, $2.50 per day.
Desk sergeants, first year, $1,020 per year.
Desk sergeants, second year, $1,080 per year.

Engineer's Department—
Chief engineer, who shall also perform all the duties heretofore performed by the superintendent of sewers, $2,500 per year.

CITY ORDINANCES.

First assistant engineer, $1,500 per year.
That the office of second assistant engineer be and the same is hereby abolished.
Chief draughtsman in the engineer's office, $1,200 per year.
That the office of assistant draughtsman be and the same is hereby abolished.
That the office of rodman and chainman be and the same is hereby abolished.
One inspector of sewers, $1,200 per year.
One clerk, $900 per year.
Engineer steam road roller, $3 per day for each day actually employed.

Miscellaneous—

Inspector of provisions, $1,080 per year.
Assistant jailor, $1,020 per year.
Janitor, City Hall, $780 per year.
Park keeper, $720 per year.
Police court clerk, $960 per year.
Recorder's clerk, $1,200 per year.
That the office of the recorder's typewriter and office boy be and the same are hereby abolished.
Sanitary inspector, $1,200 per year.
Sexton, $1,200 per year, which shall be in full for his compensation, and all moneys received by him for the sale of burial lots, or from any other source, shall be paid by him into the city treasury.
That the office of superintendent of sewers be and the same is hereby abolished.
Superintendent of waterworks, $1,800 per year.
Supervisor of streets, $1,800 per year.
Deputy treasurer, who shall also hereafter discharge and perform all the duties heretofore

See Revised Ordinances, p. 362.

discharged and performed by the license inspector, $1,500 per year.

That the office of license inspector be and the same is hereby abolished.

Water master, who shall also discharge and perform all the duties heretofore discharged and performed by the land and water commissioner, $1,500.00 per year.

The office of watermaster's foreman is hereby abolished.

Such salaries as are fixed by the year, month or day shall be paid in equal installments out of the city treasury at the end of each and every month, and the salaries herein fixed shall remain as the salaries of the officers and employees herein named until changed by the city council.

See Revised Ordinances, p. 362.

Sec. 2. All ordinances or parts of ordinances in conflict with this ordinance are hereby repealed.

Sec. 3. This ordinance to take effect and be in force from and after its passage and approval.

Passed by the city council of Salt Lake City, Territory of Utah, January 16th 1894, and referred to the mayor for his approval.

[Approved the 19th day of January, A. D., 1894.]

[Amended May 31st, 1894.]

ENGINEERS' AT SEWER PUMP.

AN ORDINANCE AMENDING SECTION 1, CHAPTER 38, OF THE REVISED ORDINANCES OF SALT LAKE CITY OF 1892.

Section 1. Be it ordained by the city council of Salt Lake City, Territory of Utah:

See Revised Ordinances p. 361.

That section 1, of chapter 38, of the revised ordinances of said city, of 1892, be amended by striking out of line 90, of said section, "$100" after the word "pump" and before the word "per," and inserting in place thereof "$87.50," and by striking out of line 92 in said section "$75" after the word "pump" and before the word "per" and inserting instead thereof "$67.50."

See Revised Ordinances, p. 364.

Sec. 2. This ordinance shall take effect and be in force from and after its approval.

Passed by the city council of Salt Lake City, Territory of Utah, September 25th, 1894, and referred to the mayor for his approval.

Approved the 29th day of September, A. D. 1894.

CHAPTER XXVI.

TREASURER—ASSESSOR.

AN ORDINANCE AUTHORIZING AND EMPOWERING THE TREASURER OF SALT LAKE CITY TO DISCHARGE THE DUTIES THAT WERE HERETOFORE PERFORMED BY THE ASSESSOR OF SAID CITY.

SECTION 1. Be it ordained by the city council of Salt Lake City, Territory of Utah:

That the treasurer of Salt Lake City be and is hereby empowered and authorized, where a special levy of a tax has been made by the city council to make any local improvement, for said treasurer to make the lists, maps and plats, as may be required by the ordinances of said city, make all entries and extensions necessary and proper for said purpose, and assess all property upon which any such levy has been made; and perform and discharge all the duties in such cases which were performed under the laws of the territory and ordinances of said city, by the city assessor prior to the office of assessor of said city being abolished.

Sec. 2. This ordinance to take effect and be in force from and after its approval.

Passed by the city council of Salt Lake City, Territory of Utah, March 3, 1893, and referred to the mayor for his approval.

[Approved the 4th day of March, .A.D. 1993.]

CHAPTER XXVII.

TAX LEVY FOR 1893.

AN ORDINANCE FIXING THE RATE AND LEVYING THE TAX ON THE ASSESSED VALUE ON THE REAL AND PERSONAL ESTATE AND PROPERTY OF SALT LAKE CITY FOR THE YEAR 1893.

SECTION 1. Be it ordained by the city council of Salt Lake City, Territory of Utah:

That there is hereby levied, and the county assessor and collector is hereby directed to levy and collect on the assessed value of all real estate, improvements and personal estate and property in Salt Lake City, for the year A.D. 1893, the sum of 5 mills on the dollar.

Sec. 2. This ordinance shall be in force from and after its approval.

Passed by the city council of Salt Lake City, Territory of Utah, June 30, 1893, and referred to the mayor for his approval.

[Approved the first day of July, A.D. 1893.]

TAX LEVY FOR 1894.

AN ORDINANCE LEVYING THE TAX ON THE ASSESSED VALUE OF THE TAXABLE PROPERTY WITHIN SALT LAKE CITY, FOR THE YEAR A. D. 1894.

SECTION 1. Be it ordained by the city council of Salt Lake City, Territory of Utah:

That there is hereby levied and the county assessor is hereby authorized to levy and the county collector to collect on the assessed value of all real estate improvements, personal estate and taxable property in Salt Lake City for the year A. D. 1894, the sum of 6½ mills on the dollar, as provided by resolution of said council June 29th, 1894.

Sec. 2. This ordinance to take effect and be in force from and after its approval.

Passed by the council of Salt Lake City, Territory of Utah, July 17th, 1894, and referred to the mayor for his approval.

[Approved the 18th day of July A. D. 1894.]

WARRANTS IN PAYMENT OF TAXES.

AN ORDINANCE PROVIDING FOR THE PAYMENT OF CITY TAXES WITH CITY WARRANTS.

SECTION 1. Be it ordained by the city council of Salt Lake City:

That the county collector shall receive city warrants in lieu of cash for city taxes, and the said collector is hereby authorized to issue his receipt for said city taxes upon the receipt of said city warrants.

Sec. 2 This ordinance to be in force from and after its passage and approval.

Passed by the city council of Salt Lake City, Territory of Utah, September 8th, 1893, and referred to the mayor for his approval.

[Approved the 11th day of September, A.D. 1893.]

CHAPTER XXVIII.

WATER RATES.

AN ORDINANCE ABOLISHING THE OFFICE OF ASSESSOR AND COLLECTOR OF WATER RATES AND PROVIDING FOR THE ASSESSMENT AND COLLECTION OF THE SAME.

SECTION 1. Be it ordained by the city council of Salt Lake City, Territory of Utah:

That the office of assessor and collector of water rates be and the same is hereby abolished.

Sec. 2. That hereafter the superintendent of waterworks shall visit each and every house in said city where water pipes have been laid, and assess each water taker for the amount of water so taken, in accordance with the provisions of chapter 55 of the Revised Ordinances of said city of 1892.

Should the superintendent of waterworks be unable to make the assessment herein required in person, he is hereby authorized to employ, by and with the advice and consent of the city council, some suitable person to make said assessment, and such person so employed shall receive as compensation for his services the sum of three dollars per day for each day's work actually performed by him.

Sec. 3. That when said assessment is completed, the assessment list or books shall be delivered to the city treasurer of the city, who shall proceed to collect the amounts of the water rate so assessed, as provided in the aforesaid ordinance.

Sec. 4. The city treasurer is hereby authorized and directed to issue to the persons now having credit in their favor on the books of the collector of water rates, a certificate for the amount of such credit, which certificate shall be called water script, and cancel the account of such person on said books, upon the issuance of said script, said script to be received in payment of water rates by said treasurer.

Sec 5. This ordinance to take effect and be in force from and after its approval.

Passed by the city council of Salt Lake City, Territory of Utah, March 27th, 1894, and referred to the mayor for his approval; and within the time prescribed by law, he having failed to approve or disapprove of the same, the said ordinance became valid and of full effect.

ASSESSMENT OF WATER RATES.

AN ORDINANCE AMENDING SECTION 8 OF AN ORDINANCE ENTITLED "AN ORDINANCE IN RELATION TO THE SALT LAKE CITY WATER WORKS," APPROVED JULY 1ST, 1892.

Be it ordained by the city council of Salt Lake City, Territory of Utah:

That section 8 of an ordinance entitled "An ordinance in relation to the Salt Lake City waterworks," approved July 1st, 1892, be and the same is hereby amended by adding at the end of said section the following:

See Revised Ordinances, p. 496

Provided, that in all cases where there is but one service pipe to any building, that the owner or agent of said building shall pay for all water used in or about the said building, supplied through said pipe, and upon failure to pay the same or any part thereof, the treasurer of Salt Lake City is hereby authorized and directed to turn the water off from said building, as provided in the ordinance to which this is an amendment.

See Revised Ordinances, p. 496.

This ordinance to take effect and be in force from and after its approval.

Passed by the city council of Salt Lake City, Territory of Utah, July 10th, 1894, and referred to the mayor for his approval.

[Approved the 11th day of July, A.D. 1894.]

Territory of Utah, } ss.
City and County of Salt Lake. }

I, Gustave H. Backman, city recorder in and for said city, do hereby certify that the foregoing fifty-four Ordinances are true and correct copies of all Ordinances of Salt Lake City passed from December 13th, 1892, to and including October 4th, 1894.

{SEAL} Witness my hand and the corporate seal of Salt Lake City, this 5th day of October, 1894.

Gustave H. Backman, City Recorder.

INDEX.

A

	Chapter.	Page
Affidavit to claims	3	11
Affidavit to payrolls	18	72
Assessor, treasurer perform duties of	26	101
Assessor and collector of water rates, abolished	28	104
Assessment of water rates	28	106

B

Barbed wire fences	10	60
Bathing resort, franchise for water pipes, H. M. Bacon	8	55
Billiards and pool, prohibiting boys in saloons	24	94
Bonfires on pavements	21	78
Bonds, confirmation to Blair & Co.	1	6
Bonds, confirmation to Blair & Co.	1	7
Bonds, issue of $800,000	1	3
Bonds, employees and clerks	2	10
Boys not allowed in saloons	24	94
Butchers' License	16	68

C

Cable railway franchise, H. M. McCartney et al	8	24
Cable railway franchise, Otto Stallman et al	8	33
Cattle, how kept (milk license)	17	70
Charges, city engineer	5	13
Charges, deposit on application for franchise	9	58
Charges, hack drivers	13	64
Chief of police—ex-officio jailor	20	75
Claims, sworn to	3	11
Clerks and employees, give bonds	2	10
Compensation (see salaries)	25	96
Compensation of oil inspector	14	65

D

Deposit on application for franchise	9	58
Detective or special police	21	76

	Chapter	Page
Districts, paving	19	73
Districts, sprinkling	22	83
Districts, sewer	23	88
Driver of Hack, etc.	13	63

E

Electric franchises.
S. F. Walker	8	40
R. M. Jones	8	43
Salt Lake & Ogden Gas & Electric Light Company	8	48
Rocky Mountain Bell Telephone Company	8	51

Electric railway franchises.
Salt Lake City Railroad Company	8	17
Salt Lake Rapid Transit Company	8	20
H. M. McCartney et al	8	24
Wm. H. Rowe et al	8	28
Otto Stallman et al	8	33
Employment office (changes in license)	4	12
Engineer's charges	5	13
Engineers at sewer pump, salaries	29	99
Excavations in streets	21	79

F

Fees, city engineer for surveying, etc.	5	13
Fees, oil inspector	14	65
Fences, hight of	10	59
Fences, barbed wire prohibited	10	60
Food and drink (milk ordinance)	17	70
Fire department, number of men	6	15
Fire hydrants, injury to	7	16
Franchises, deposit on application for	9	58

Franchises
Salt Lake City Railroad Company	8	17
Salt Lake Rapid Transit Company	8	20
H. M. McCartney et al	8	24
Wm. H. Rowe et al	8	28
Otto Stallman et al	8	33
Salt Lake & Los Angeles Railway Company	8	38
S F. Walker	8	40
R. M. Jones	8	43
Salt Lake & Ogden Gas & Electric Light Company	8	48
Rocky Mountain Bell Telephone Company	8	51
Harvey M. Bacon	8	55

G

	Chapter	Page
Garbage, disposal of.	11	61
Garnishment, waiver of exemption	12	62
Gas (see franchises)	8	—

H

Hack ordinance.	13	63
Hack drivers' charges.	13	64
Heating, etc.		
Franchise S. F. Walker	8	40
Franchise R. M. Jones	8	43
Franchise Salt Lake & Ogden Gas & Electric Light Company.	8	48
Hight of fences	10	59

I

Inspector of oils, compensation	14	65
Inspector of meat and live stock	15	66
Inspection of meat, places of.	15	66

J

Jailor, chief ex-officio	20	75
Jailor, assistant	20	75

L

Licenses.		
Reduction for employment office	4	12
Butchers, slaughterers, etc.	16	68
Milk	17	70
Salt Lake City Railway Company, $25 per car	—	17
Salt Lake Rapid Transit Company, $25 per car	—	20
Light and heat.		
Franchise to R. M. Jones	8	43
Franchise Salt Lake & Ogden Gas & Electric Light Company.	8	48
Live Stock Inspection	15	66

M

Meat and live stock inspection	15	66
Meat, sale of.	16	68
Milk, license	17	70

O

Official bonds	2	10
Oath to claims	3	11

	Chapter.	Page.
Oath to payrolls	18	72
Oils, inspector of	14	65

P

	Chapter.	Page.
Pavement, bonfires prohibited on	21	78
Pavement, repair of	21	81
Paving districts	19	73
Payrolls verified	18	72
Police, chief as ex-officio jailor	20	75
Police department, number of men	20	76
Police, special or detective	20	76
Power, heating, etc.		
Franchise S. F. Walker	8	40
Franchise R. M. Jones	8	43
Franchise Salt Lake & Ogden Gas & Electric Light Company	8	48

R

	Chapter.	Page.
Railroad Franchises.		
Salt Lake City Railroad Company	8	17
Salt Lake Rapid Transit Company	8	20
H. M McCartney et al	8	24
Wm. H. Rowe et al	8	28
Otto Stallman et al	8	33
Salt Lake & Los Angeles Railway Company	8	38

S

	Chapter.	Page.
Salaries	25	96
Inspector of Oils	14	65
Inspector of Meats and Live Stock	15	66
Engineers at Sewer pump	25	99
Saloons, boys not allowed in	24	94
Salt Lake and Los Angeles Railway Company Franchise	8	38
Sanitarium Franchise to H. M. Bacon	8	55
Slaughterers, Etc. License	16	68
Stock Inspector	15	66
Streets.		
Bonfires prohibited on paved	21	78
Change in name of Green Street	21	79
Excavations	21	79
Repair of Pavements	21	81
Street Railway Franchises.		
Salt Lake City Railroad Company	8	17
Salt Lake Rapid Transit Company	8	20
H. M. McCartney et al	8	24
Wm. H. Rowe et al	8	28
Otto Stallman et al	8	33

INDEX

	Chapter	Page
Surveying, Charges for	5	13
Sprinkling District No. 3	22	83
Sprinkling District No. 4	22	84
Sprinkling District No. 5	22	85
Sprinkling District No. 6	22	86
Sewer Districts	23	88
Sewer pump, engineer of	25	90

T

	Chapter	Page
Tax Levy for 1893	27	102
Tax Levy for 1894	27	102
Taxes, payment in warrants	27	103
Telephone and Telegraph (see franchises)		
Treasurer perform duties of Assessor	26	101

V

	Chapter	Page
Vehicles (in relation to Driver, etc.)	26	63

W

	Chapter	Page
Waiver of exemption from garnishment	12	62
Warrants received for city taxes	27	103
Water rates, assessment of	28	104
Water rates	28	106
Water pipes, franchise	8	55
West Capitol street	21	79
Wire fences prohibited	10	60

www.ingramcontent.com/pod-product-compliance
Lightning Source LLC
Chambersburg PA
CBHW020145170426
43199CB00010B/892